English-Only Teachers in Mixed-Language Classrooms | A SURVIVAL GUIDE

English-Only Teachers in Mixed-Language Classrooms A SURVIVAL GUIDE

Joanne Yatvin

HEINEMANN
Portsmouth, NH

Heinemann

361 Hanover Street
Portsmouth, NH 03801–3912
www.heinemann.com

Offices and agents throughout the world

Library of Congress Cataloging-in-Publication Data
Yatvin, Joanne.
    English-only teachers in mixed-language classrooms : a survival guide / Joanne Yatvin.
        p. cm.
    ISBN-13: 978-0-325-00969-8 (pbk. : alk. paper)
    ISBN-10: 0-325-00969-4
    1. English language—Study and teaching—Foreign speakers.   2. English teachers—Training of—United States.   3. Language teachers—Training of—United States.   4. Mainstreaming in education.   I. Title.
PE1128.A2Y37   2007
428.2′4—dc22   2006038450

Editor: Jim Strickland
Production: Lynne Costa
Cover design: Jenny Jensen Greenleaf
Cover illustration: © Getty Images/PhotoDisc 107013
Typesetter: House of Equations, Inc.
Manufacturing: Steve Bernier

Printed in the United States of America on acid-free paper
11 10 09 08   VP   2 3 4 5

For the men in my life:
Jack Goldberg, my father
Milton Yatvin, my husband
and
my sons, Alan, Bruce, and Richard

Contents

Acknowledgments   ix

Introduction: The American Classroom Today   1

1: Basic Beliefs and Guidelines   5

2: Preparing for a Mixed-Language Classroom   12

3: Welcoming ELLs into the Classroom   24

4: Beginning English Instruction   31

5: Teaching Reading and Writing   43

6: Content Learning   66

7: ELLs and English-Speaking Students Learning Together   83

8: Providing Further Support for ELLs   101

Acknowledgments

First in line for my gratitude are the English language learners and their classmates at Alder and Davis elementary schools in the Reynolds School District in Gresham, Oregon, and their counterparts whom I met earlier in classrooms in Portland, Beaverton, and North Clackamas. These bright, friendly, and hardworking children were both the inspiration and the source of my understanding of teaching and learning in mixed-language classrooms.

Close behind them in deserving thanks are the outstanding teachers whose classrooms I concentrated on: Linda Spangler, Heather Smith, Sharla Sanford, Emma Harris, and Sheryl Lindley. I also wish to acknowledge their principals, Susan Dunn and Rick Fraisse, for opening their schools to me and assisting me in getting the observation time, photographs, and parent permissions I needed. Educational assistant, Jan Fentz, helped explain to me what was going on in classrooms when I just didn't get it.

Many others played important roles in the creation of this book: Although I have never met Marcia Brechtel, the teacher who created Project GLAD (Guided Literacy Acquisition Design), I and thousands of teachers are indebted to her for her insightful and effective guidance for teaching English and content subjects in regular classrooms. I want to thank my friend Anne Kolibaba, who told me about the fine work being done with English language learners at Alder School and got me through the door, and Katherine Kondyllis, the ESL coordinator there, who led me to the kind of teachers I wanted to see. I also want to thank Deb O'Dell and Lara Smith, the skilled instructors of the GLAD workshop I participated in before researching this book. And I cannot neglect to thank Lois Bridges, my former editor, for suggesting that this type of book was needed and encouraging me to write it.

At Heinemann, my editor, Jim Strickland, has been a wise and efficient advocate. He has treated me and my work gently, helped to get me organized, and pushed to get the book out the way I wanted it and ahead of schedule. Lynne Costa, my production editor, also devoted herself to getting the book out quickly without any diminution of quality.

Although I am usually silent about the constant support of my family, Milton, Alan, Bruce, and Richard, I want to admit here how much they do to encourage me, take over my responsibilities, and calm my worries, so that I can write.

Finally, I want to acknowledge my daughter, the late Lillian Aked Yatvin, who was—and always will be—my model of courage and honesty. She "walked the walk" that I often only "talk." Along with the supportive presence of my husband, her memory keeps me doing the work I've always wanted to do but never had the confidence or perseverance for when I was young.

—Joanne Yatvin

Acknowledgments

English-Only Teachers in
Mixed-Language Classrooms | **A SURVIVAL GUIDE**

Poster of all the languages and cultures at Alder School, Gresham, Oregon

Introduction
The American Classroom Today

Languages and Cultures at Alder School

A merican classrooms are not what they were fifty years ago, or even ten years ago. Along with the imposition of external standards, federal demands for adequate yearly progress for all groups of students, and the pressure to use one-size-fits-all textbooks, the makeup of classroom populations has changed significantly. Long after the Supreme Court called for school desegregation in 1954, families were held in certain parts of the country and in certain types of communities by social class, race, and ethnicity. As recently as the 1990s, Hispanic populations were concentrated in California, Texas, Illinois, New York, and Florida, the traditional gateways for Hispanic immigration. Immigrants from Eastern Europe were also concentrated in the urban areas of the East and West coasts, through which they had entered this country. And refugees from oppressive regimes and wars in the Far East settled where their American benefactors lived and supported them.

Today, however, the patterns for most of these minority groups have changed, and in some cases the population scatterings do not even constitute patterns at all. Hispanics, the largest immigrant population in the United States, make up at least five percent of the population in twenty-five of our states. Many Hispanic families no longer live in traditional ethnic neighborhoods, but in what were always white, working-class neighborhoods throughout the country and in rural areas where year-round agricultural and manufacturing jobs are available. Concentrations of European and Asian minorities are harder to pinpoint, but they, too, are moving out of cities and into suburban areas as their financial status improves and new ethnic communities are formed.

As a result of these population movements, midwestern, southeastern, mountain, and plains states, long accustomed to a homogeneous Caucasian population or a black-white mix, are experiencing an increasing influx of foreign-born families. For the first time, suburban and even rural schools throughout the country are absorbing varying numbers of children whose native language is not English, and in many places these newcomers bring not just one new language into a classroom but a variety of unrelated languages.

Moreover, some children who come from impoverished or war-torn countries have either never been enrolled in any school or attended school only irregularly. Although they are as physically and mentally capable as their American-born classmates, and of the right ages for upper-elementary or high school grades, they cannot yet read, write, or do math in any language.

Clearly, placing these children in classrooms where teachers are not prepared to teach them—or even communicate with them—is neither sound educational practice nor humane treatment. But that is what is happening. With money so tight as the result of increased federal demands for testing, tutoring, and transferring students to other schools, few public schools receiving English language learners for the first time are able to hire English as a second language teachers or translators to train classroom teachers. Nor can they provide small introductory classes for incoming students. Thus, English language learners are left to learn—or not learn—through full immersion in regular classrooms at all levels.

Not only are such situations bad for English language learners, but they are also bad for classroom teachers. These mostly monolingual teachers are expected to teach their new students to speak, read, and write English and to prepare them to take federally mandated tests in content subjects, given in English, in their second year of attendance. Looking further into the difficulties of these new mixed-language classrooms, we may wonder if the English-speaking students are not also being harmed. With teachers overburdened, undersupported by their schools, and continually anxious about preserving their jobs and professional reputations, how high can the quality of instruction for everyone be?

The purpose of this book is to suggest a range of basic survival strategies, materials, and activities for English-only teachers and English language learners in mixed-language classrooms. Although government entities at all levels have abandoned their responsibilities to children and teachers, this book offers practical suggestions to help teachers fill the void. Through its eight brief, yet detailed chapters, this book addresses the problems of organizing a classroom and teaching for full participation of students whose native languages and cultures are different from those of English-speaking students born and raised in this country.

English-Only Teachers in Mixed-Language Classrooms begins with an overview of theory of second language learning and a set of practical guidelines for classroom teaching in Chapter 1. From there, Chapter 2 moves into the business of preparing the classroom and its English-speaking students for the arrival of students who may speak little or no English. Chapter 3 deals with welcoming such students, orienting them to the classroom and its ways, and helping them to get through their first rough days of severely limited communication. It also includes directions for training student guides to familiarize new students with the places, people, and ways of doing things in their new school.

Chapter 4 explicitly details beginning oral instruction for students who speak little or no English. It explains how other students can help newcomers and how teachers can most efficiently and effectively ready them to work with their English-speaking classmates on grade-level academics.

Chapter 5, dealing with teaching reading and writing, contains many suggestions for adapting the work English-speaking students are doing to fit the capabilities of English language learners.

Chapter 6 explores the range of whole-class work in the content areas at different grade levels, using the philosophy and techniques taught by teacher Marcia Brechtel of Fountain Valley, California, as part of her Project GLAD (Guided Language Acquisition Design). All the teachers whom I observed in the writing of this book had received training in GLAD, and after only a few classroom visits, I decided to enroll in the training program as well.

Chapter 7 describes a variety of classroom grouping practices that allow English language learners to work with and learn from English-speaking students. It also discusses the need for teachers to instruct English language learners individually and in separate small groups at times in order to help those who are having problems and advance those who are making rapid progress.

Finally, Chapter 8 returns to the social and psychological concerns of English language learners and their families. It suggests ways for teachers to include and honor their native languages and cultures in the classroom and to encourage them to feel pride in their origins. This chapter also discusses how teachers can form relationships with parents, drawing them into the classroom and enlisting them as partners in their children's education.

Throughout the book I have taken the liberty of shortening the term *English language learners* to *ELLs* in order not to have to repeat the long form in nearly every sentence. This practice certainly should not confuse the reader, and I sincerely hope that it does not offend anyone either. More important, I have taken a perspective that could be characterized as envisioning worst-case scenarios. In describing various classroom situations for teachers and students to deal with, I deliberately made them as difficult as possible. I posited teachers who do not know even a few words of another language, large classes with several English language learners in them, new students who know little or no English, a dribbling in of newcomers over the course of the school year, and a variety of native languages and cultures in a classroom. By taking this extreme perspective, I was able to describe maximum support strategies and cover most contingencies. If the situation in your classroom turns out to be not nearly as challenging as the ones described, not only will you feel fortunate, but you will also have more than enough information and creative ideas to teach all students effectively.

Basic Beliefs and Guidelines

1

What I Learned from Experience

A long time ago when I started teaching English as a second language (ESL) to middle schoolers in Puerto Rico, I didn't have a clue about what I should be doing. All my previous teaching had been in elementary classrooms where the native language of all my students was English. A few years later I taught ESL to graduate students from many different countries at the University of Wisconsin. I was then working on a PhD that included courses in applied English linguistics, which is an elegant way of saying second language teaching. Theoretically, I was well prepared, but I was still naïve about the practical, social, and psychological needs of my students, who were strangers in a strange land.

With knowledge of ESL pedagogy and a better understanding of the way the English language works, it is not surprising that I did a much better job of teaching English my second time around. But I think there were other, more important factors affecting the progress of my grad students than my ability to teach: their maturity, their strong motivation, and the English language environment they were living in. They understood that they needed to learn English quickly and thoroughly to be allowed to proceed with their studies at the university and go on to their chosen careers. And, for the most part, they had to use English to communicate with the people around them. Most of my middle schoolers had had no such needs or any great interest in learning English. They lived in an environment where they spoke Spanish every waking hour of the day, except for the one they spent with me, and they were not looking ahead to a time when they might want to seek jobs on the U.S. mainland, where bilingualism would be an asset.

These early classroom experiences helped shape my own philosophy of second language teaching and learning, but I was also influenced by my experiences living as an English-only speaker in Spanish-speaking Puerto Rico and, years later, in Dutch-speaking Belgium and Hebrew-speaking Israel. Out of necessity, I learned to communicate fast—if not correctly—in the languages of those countries and to solve the problems of daily living. It didn't matter that store clerks occasionally snickered at me. Using a combination of the local languages, English, and gestures, I was able to get what I wanted.

While living in Belgium, I experienced second language teaching and learning from a third perspective, which also influenced my thinking. As part of my dissertation research, I visited thirty elementary and secondary schools in Belgium, Germany, and the Netherlands to observe beginning classes in English and French. What I saw was that students' accomplishments in the language being taught varied widely from school to school. In keeping with what I had been taught in my university courses, I realized that those variations were more the results of teaching methods, the intrinsic motivation of the students, and the characteristics of their native languages[1] than of individual differences in students' ability. I still think that assessment was correct.

Admittedly, I cannot translate my past experiences directly to the situations of students or teachers in American schools today. Both the physical and psychological factors are significantly different when the teacher and most of the students speak one language, a few students

---

1. Because Dutch is closer to English than French or German in its grammar and pronunciation, Dutch-speaking students have an easier time learning English as a second language.

English-Only Teachers in Mixed-Language Classrooms

speak other languages, and those few are also living in a foreign environment where they don't know the rules of the social game. Still, I believe that the essential principles of the English language teaching and learning, and human behavior are the same today as they were then, and that they can be developed into everyday practices for classrooms with an English-only teacher, a few ELLs, and a preponderance of English-speaking students.

More recently, I have been spending considerable time as an observer in elementary mixed-language classrooms in Oregon, watching skilled English-only teachers and ELLs at work. These experiences have confirmed my philosophy and added many practical ideas about effective classroom activities. Bringing everything together, I have developed a statement of theory and a set of practical guidelines for teaching and learning in mixed-language classrooms today, designed to help everyone in them survive and prosper. That theory and those guidelines follow.

A Theory of Second Language Learning

The best way for learners to acquire a second language is to live it. When learners listen, speak, read, and write in a new language daily, its elements have meaning and become automatic in use. Learners also begin to think in that language. An important component of living a language is the external and internal motivation that impels learners to want to communicate with those around them, to belong to a peer group, and to obtain the social, educational, civic, and professional benefits that accrue to competent users of a language.

Learners function best in an environment where there are rewards for efforts to communicate but no penalties for errors or weaknesses. In such an environment there is also freedom for experimentation and mixing in words and expressions from one's native language with those of the second language when necessary.

The natural progression of learning a second language is imitating spoken words and phrases, understanding those spoken by others, experimenting with speech, writing what one knows from oral interaction, reading familiar language, and finally moving beyond the familiar into areas of need and interest in speech, writing, and reading.

The Difference Between Theory and Reality

The trouble with any theory is that it presumes ideal conditions. This one presumes *living a language*, which means functioning socially, physically, economically, psychologically, and politically in a foreign environment, immersed in its demands, encouragements, benefits, and continuing practice opportunities. Unfortunately, school is not such an environment for ELLs, and neither is their home nor their community. All of those places offer only a part of what a learner needs, and at the same time they give him convenient escape hatches to avoid using English, such as interacting with his native language peers almost exclusively. When we try to translate ELL theory into classroom practice, we not only have to adjust our expectations downward for motivation and the amount of language use but also have to settle for a simulated environment that may not be either as forgiving or as stimulating as life in the real world. To help teachers make the most of what is possible in schools, I offer the following guidelines for teaching English to ELLs.

Guidelines for Teaching ELLs in a Mixed-Language Classroom

1. ELLs need a welcome kit upon their entrance to a mixed-language classroom. No teacher has enough time during those first few days of class to explain everything an ELL needs to know about getting along in the school and the classroom. A kit with vital information for the student and her parents—in English and, if possible, also in her native language—should be immediately available. The kit should contain, at the very least, an illustrated vocabulary card designed to meet a student's basic everyday needs, such as getting food and finding a toilet. It should also contain necessary information about the school and the classroom for the student and her parents.

2. As soon as possible, the teacher should have a private conversation with an entering ELL to find out about his educational and cultural background and the extent of his knowledge of English, and to acquaint him with classroom routines and rituals. At this conversation, an English-speaking student who will act as the ELL's guide should also be present in order to learn how he can

English-Only Teachers in Mixed-Language Classrooms

support the newcomer over the first week or two through further explanations, demonstrations, and practice.

3. All supply and work areas of the classroom should be labeled with English terms and pictures or symbols that explain their purposes and, if possible, illustrate their rules for use, such as how many people may work in an area at one time.

4. During the first few weeks that an ELL is in the classroom, the teacher should concentrate on oral teaching of everyday vocabulary and commonly used sentence structures. Concentrating on reading and writing and academic content comes later when the student has become familiar with everyday school and classroom operations. While teachers may also introduce the written forms of vocabulary words they teach, and have ELLs practice saying them, they should not expect these students to be able to read those words without an accompanying picture or to spell them until after more systematic literacy instruction has begun.

5. When the time comes for an ELL to participate in the grade-level content curriculum, directions for doing classroom work should be presented in as many modes and contexts as possible. Teachers need to form the habit of accompanying oral teaching with pictures, diagrams, examples, and step-by-step instructions and be willing to repeat them as necessary. In addition, for unfamiliar classroom activities, ELLs should be partnered with English-speaking students who know what to do.

6. Lower-level English trade books and textbooks, reference books with the basic material of content courses, and English picture dictionaries should be available in sufficient quantities for ELLs. Although ELLs in the upper-elementary grades should not have to suffer through first-grade primers and alphabet books in their reading groups, they are going to need interesting material that has fewer new vocabulary words and simpler sentence structures for reading on their own, and simpler subject matter materials for independent research in science, social studies, and other subjects.

7. Teachers at all levels who have ELLs in their classrooms should use rhymes, games, chants, songs, raps, and poems for teaching more frequently than they would if all their students were native English

speakers. Many of these easily remembered and engaging oral forms can be created by the teacher (and later by the class) for the purpose of learning new words, meanings, and information.

8. Teachers in the elementary grades should use a whole language approach to teaching reading and writing to ELLs rather than a phonics approach. Although ELLs may be able to pronounce words by sounding them out phonetically, they will not comprehend text unless most of the words are already in their spoken vocabulary. They will also need to preview materials thoroughly before attempting to read them, and review them afterward to ensure understanding. Early writing experiences for ELLs should be short and simple and should follow patterns they are already familiar with.

9. Teachers should include English language versions of some of the best-loved stories from ELL students' native cultures when they read aloud to the whole class and, if they are available, provide copies printed in the original language for students to peruse before and after hearing the English versions. Teachers should encourage ELLs to reread English language books they are familiar with and enjoy and bring native language books from home to serve as links between their cultures and the new school culture.

10. Since ELLs learn best through authentic practice, rather than workbook exercises or drills, teachers should provide as many opportunities as possible for students to speak or write what they want to say (rather than words or sentences from a prepared list or worksheet), allowing them to use words from their native language whenever they don't yet know the English forms.

11. Grammatical correctness and complete sentences are not important in the early stages of second language learning. As long as ELLs are communicating understandably, teachers should not correct errors or slips back into their native language. However, when teachers hear the same kinds of mistakes over and over, they should plan to introduce the conventional English oral forms in individual conferences or small-group meetings.

12. Both external motivation and internal motivation are necessary for ELLs to be successful at learning a new language. In school the

strongest external motivations for ELLs are the approval and encouragement of their teachers, classmates, and parents and the reward of raised status among them. Their strongest internal motivations are increased self-esteem and the need to communicate, work, and play with their classmates.

13. A classroom that is hospitable to ELLs' native languages and cultures will give them the confidence and self-respect necessary to approach all learning challenges positively. If students feel that their native language and culture are considered less worthy of respect in their classroom than English, they may become resentful and resist learning English and subject matter taught in English. Thus, it would be a good idea for the teacher and the English-speaking students to learn some words from the native languages of ELLs and to experience stories, poems, songs, and art from their cultures.

14. Mastery of everyday oral communication does not mean that ELLs will be able to read and write academic English without support. Most experts say that attaining true academic fluency takes five to seven years for ELLs. Fortunately, the younger the student is at school entrance, the shorter is his road to academic competence.

Throughout this book, the theory and guidelines described in this chapter—though not often mentioned specifically—consistently underlie the methods, activities, and materials suggested for instruction, practice, and evaluation of student progress. From here on we shall be looking at teaching and learning through a pragmatic lens, thinking of what you as a teacher can do with the time and energy you have in any busy classroom and of the specific needs and interests of all your students.

Preparing for a Mixed-Language Classroom

2

If you knew in July that five Spanish-speaking children would be part of your new class on the first day of school, I'm guessing you would work during the summer to get your classroom ready for them. Chances are, however, that until they walk through the door, you won't know your English language learners are coming, that they'll arrive one at a time over the course of the year, and that only two of them will speak the same language, which probably won't be Spanish. Your best bet, then, would be to make a plan of action for integrating ELLs into your classroom near the end of the summer break while you are making all the usual preparations for the school year to come.

Before you make that plan, however, take an informal survey of the school and the neighborhood. Here are the kinds of questions you'll want to ask yourself, the principal, other teachers, and community agencies:

How many ELLs are already enrolled at your school?
How many are in the grade level right below yours?
Are there large numbers of houses or apartments available that
　　might attract recent immigrants?
How many ELLs are typically placed in any one classroom?

In general, do the ELLs who enter your school know some English when they arrive?

How well do the present ELLs function in the school community?

Do ELLs' parents come to school conferences and participate in school events?

In general, how well do these parents speak and/or understand English?

Is there a particular ethnic community growing in your school neighborhood?

What agencies and public services are in place to help families that are not familiar with the ways of an American community and not conversant in English?

The answers to these questions will give you a good idea of what to expect in the near future and guide your planning for the physical features of your room, curricular modifications, selection of teaching and recreational materials, organization of students for learning, and dealing with emergencies.

Physical Aspects of the Classroom

As I stated in the introduction, this book assumes worst-case scenarios so that teachers will be able to deal with whatever comes their way. Part of the worst-case scenario on preparedness is that your school is totally ill equipped to accommodate the needs of ELLs. There is no ESL teacher, no school orientation program, no staff members who speak the students' native languages, and no contingency fund to tap into for any of these things. Except for empathetic colleagues, who are there for you even in worst-case scenarios, you are on your own.

One thing every teacher can do is to set up his classroom so that it will work for the English-speaking students now and for the ELLs to come. This way, even if a few minor changes are necessary later, neither the students nor the teacher will feel that their familiar classroom world is being torn up and rebuilt for newcomers. The physical features of the classroom and its instructional and recreational contents will vary with the grade level, but the same types of things have to be considered and planned for at every level.

Although most teachers have little say in selecting the furniture for their classrooms, you may already have desks that have flat tops and can be moved together for group work. If you are lucky enough to have a choice, however, go for round tables, fifty-four inches in diameter, that will accommodate four to six students. They are the best furniture for any classroom because they take up less space than desks, leaving room for various kinds of movement and gatherings, and allow students to work as partners or in teams at their tables. They also happen to be much cheaper than desks, with one table costing less than two student desks. Whatever furniture you end up with should be arranged to make four to six groupings with places for six students at each group of desks or each table. The ELL-prepared teacher will leave one or two places in each grouping open at the beginning of the year for ELLs who might arrive later. In the meantime, students from other groups may use the empty spaces temporarily to allow greater flexibility in collaborative work.

This seating plan assumes that there are from twenty to thirty children in the class to begin with, and that four to six more may enter later on. (For everyone's sake, I hope there will never be thirty-six children in any elementary classroom, but remember this is a worst-case scenario.) The point of this seating plan is not only to have small groups of students working together and forming social relationships but also to have new ELLs placed where they can receive help from English-speaking students and advanced ELLs, follow their lead in routines and work procedures, and communicate with them in some manner right from the start. Although it may seem more efficient and more compassionate to put a newly arrived ELL next to another ELL who speaks the same language and has been there for a while, this practice can delay English language learning and socialization for both of them. Out of a sense of self-protection, most ELLs will choose to associate only with each other and converse only in their native language. Don't facilitate these habits by seating ELLs together and expecting them to help each other with English.

Another consideration in arranging desks or tables is maximum visibility of all wall areas. You are going to depend on charts, posters, semipermanent written material, and pictures much more than on chalkboard messages, so you want all students to be able to see them easily. It might be a good idea to reserve almost all the available wall space for these long-term items and use a pull-down screen for projecting daily messages, examples, and assignments.

Other classroom furniture need not be special, only child friendly and age appropriate. If you set up workstations, project centers, or recreational reading areas, always think in terms of two students (or multiples of two) working together.

Finally, when ELLs are part of the class, all work areas, storage spaces, and collection places for written work should be labeled with English words and explanatory pictures. Even if older ELLs can figure out what these are by watching others, they will eventually need to learn to read and say the names of these centers. If labeling every shelf, drawer, and table in an English-speaking sixth-grade classroom at the beginning of the year seems too juvenile, let it wait until ELLs arrive and then explain to everyone how labeling will help them learn English.

Gathering the Necessary Materials

When it comes to instructional materials, much more than the regular grade-level textbooks and reference books is necessary. Specifically, you will need many easy-to-read fiction and nonfiction books and a few lower-level textbooks in science, social studies, and math that cover the same topics you plan to cover in your grade-level curriculum. These books don't have to be new. With luck, you can borrow some from lower-grade teachers or rescue them from collections of old library books to be discarded. Other sources are your school library and public library, if you can negotiate a longer period of time to keep them than the usual two weeks. You will also need a couple of lower-level student dictionaries, preferably picture dictionaries, and some simple reference books. In addition, you should have a copy of the *Oxford Picture Dictionary*, which contains almost four thousand English words and thus is suitable for older ELLs. In Figure 2.1, grade 5 teacher Heather Smith is putting together her classroom library at the beginning of the school year. As you can see, she has a separate area for nonfiction books.

Because most commercially produced reference books written at a low reading level are hard to find and expensive, a good alternative

Figure 2.1   Teacher Heather Smith and her classroom library

is to have your English-speaking students produce their own reference books as they study various topics before any ELLs arrive. Later, ELLs can learn a great deal of subject matter easily by collaborating on creating these types of books with their English-speaking classmates.[1] If they are sturdily bound, these reference books will serve new ELLs for years to come.

For recreational reading, easy trade books, including high-quality picture books with little or no text, are a necessity. Illustrated informational books on any topic are especially valuable for ELLs, who must expand their vocabulary and understanding of concepts on a variety of topics as quickly as possible. Be discriminating in choosing books, however. Their language structure should be simple and the vocabulary limited and nontechnical, yet you don't want to insult students by choosing stories or topics that are suitable only for much younger children. Like your English-speaking students, fifth-grade ELLs do not want to read about bunnies or trips to the zoo. Humor, adventure, and folktales work well for any age, but don't overlook

---

1. The process of creating easy-to-read reference books is discussed in Chapter 7.

English-Only Teachers in Mixed-Language Classrooms

comic books and graphic novels. Graphic novels are a fairly recent and growing development in the publishing field that is proving to be a strong support for comprehension for both ELLs and struggling English-speaking readers. This new literary form is a full-length story told in a picture sequence, with only a little text. Thus, it is much like a comic strip, but with more of the story told in dialogue and narrative. Many graphic novels are quite sophisticated in both their language and illustrations, telling complex and nuanced stories. At the end of this chapter I supply a short list of graphic novels recommended by teachers, librarians, and reviewers.

I believe graphic novels can be a lifesaver for levels 1 and 2 ELLs and their teachers in terms of supporting reading comprehension. Students can read them independently in a reading workshop structure and later share them with their families at home. Not only does the graphic element support comprehension, but it also does a good job of explaining new vocabulary words. Although it may take you a while to convince administrators that graphic novels are a legitimate instructional tool for ELLs and slowly progressing English-speaking readers, in the meantime, you could buy a few good books of this type for recreational reading and add them to your classroom library.

If you can reserve any school funds to buy books later in the year, wait till after a few ELLs have arrived and then buy a few books in their own languages or about their cultures. Not only will they enjoy reading these books silently to themselves or aloud to other students, but they will also better appreciate their own skills and earn the respect of their classmates.

For all instructional purposes, teachers need an extensive picture file. Notice that I did not say they need it for their ELLs. Pictures help all students with vocabulary and concepts. The only difference is that when you have ELLs, your file has to be bigger and include a lot of pictures of everyday objects and situations that English-speaking students do not need. Figure 2.2 offers some examples of the general types of pictures you should collect, but you will also need pictures to fit the units in your science and social studies curriculum and the age-appropriate interests of all your students.

The number and simplicity of the pictures you collect will vary with grade level, but do not assume that older ELLs will find the names of ordinary objects too easy. Some objects, such as hair dryers or footballs, may not be common in their native environments.

Figure 2.2 Suggested picture file contents

Suggested Picture File Contents

People—different ages, races, ethnic types, and genders

Animals—wild, farm, and domestic animals

Buildings—public, religious, business, and school buildings

Foods—meats, dairy products, vegetables, fruits, and cereals

Tools—home, construction, repair, and gardening tools

Vehicles—different types of cars, trucks, boats, and planes

Clothing—seasonal, outdoor and indoor clothing, shoes, sweaters, caps, and hats

Growing things—trees, flowers, and plants

Sports and games

Home appliances and utensils

Furniture

Weather types

Brand products—food, cleaners, snacks, drinks, and clothing

Classroom objects

Geographic sites—mountains, deserts, fields, forests, towns, cities, rivers, oceans, lakes, farms, and ranches

Times of day

Toys

Personal possessions—iPods, cell phones, backpacks, purses, wallets, and watches

Since building a comprehensive picture file takes a long time, ELL-prepared teachers will start before any ELLs have arrived in their rooms and understand that they will have to continue building those files indefinitely. Good sources of pictures are the Internet, ads in ordinary magazines, and photos in specialized magazines, such as *National Geographic.* Discarded textbooks and encyclopedias can also yield a broad range of photos and drawings. If you can't find particular pictures that you need, ask a few of your artistically inclined students to draw them for you.

Depending upon the age of your students, you should have certain types of common objects in the classroom, too. In kindergarten

English-Only Teachers in Mixed-Language Classrooms

and first grade, having a playhouse with furniture, dishes, and dress-up clothes is important. It gives all children an opportunity to practice oral language connected to everyday living. Young children also benefit from having a dollhouse, a play store, a set of small plastic animals, a puppet theatre, and a collection of small replicas of objects, animals, and people. Miniature replicas of objects and creatures are useful in upper-grade classrooms, too. Having these things available encourages students to use a broader range of vocabulary and sentence structures unself-consciously in imaginative play.

All the items mentioned previously can be considered basic features of a mixed-language classroom, but there are also many other items that will help to enhance the language and content learning of your ELLs. For example, videos, filmstrips, books on tape (matched to the printed books in the classroom), board games, CDs of popular songs, movies, magazines, and daily newspapers, though costly, would be valuable tools for all students to expand their general knowledge and improve their reading.

Designing a Welcome Kit

Children who enter a classroom after the school year has begun—whether ELLs or English speakers—have many questions and concerns that the teacher has no time to discuss with them immediately. It's important to assign a temporary guide for newcomers and to prepare a welcome kit for them to help themselves. A welcome kit should contain important information about the school and the classroom for entering students and their parents. If you know that most entering ELLs will be speaking a particular language, look for a native speaker to translate the greetings and contact information into that language. At the same time, the information should be included in English, too, so that newcomers who already know English will not be insulted. Although the nature of the kit's contents will differ somewhat from school to school and classroom to classroom, the essentials are listed in Figure 2.3. The kit should be divided into two sections, the first for the student and the second for parents.

Figure 2.3   Contents of a welcome kit

Contents of an ELL Welcome Kit

For the Student

A letter of greeting to the student from the teacher

A simplified map of the school, with pictures or symbols of bathrooms, office, library, lunchroom, gym, nurse's office (if there is one), and any other place a student might need to go to alone

A set of school rules including any dress code

An eight-by-eleven-inch card with names and photos of all class members, with the photo of the child chosen to be the new student's classroom guide highlighted

An eight-by-eleven-inch necessity card with pictures and names of things a new ELL might need, such as a pencil, paper, food, and scissors

A small gift, such as a pencil, notepad, sweatband, or pair of shoelaces printed with the name of the school

For the Parents

A letter of greeting

A calendar of school events, holidays, and school breaks that includes daily opening and dismissal times

Names and phone numbers of the principal, counselor, classroom teacher, and school social worker

A list of required school supplies

Making Welcome Kits

As for the welcome kits, you should put together as much of the first one as you can before the school year begins. Using the kit you have prepared as a model, members of the class can put together other kits for additional newcomers and add things like their own pictures

English-Only Teachers in Mixed-Language Classrooms

and any new school rules or procedures. They can make the necessity cards with words and pictures and the cards with their names and photos.

In the upper grades, some students will be able to draw good maps of the school that can be duplicated. Others can sew bags or decorate envelopes to hold the kits. A child of any age can put copies of written information pages in order and insert them into new kits. When each kit is finished, adding a personal note from the student who prepared the kit to the newcomer is a nice final touch.

Preparing English-Speaking Students for New Arrivals

Sometime during the first week or two of school, you should have a discussion with your class about the likelihood of ELL newcomers arriving during the year. What you want to come out of that discussion is that it is hard—and maybe scary—to come into a new place where everyone knows each other, how to do things, where to find what they need, and when to do certain work or go certain places and you are the only one who doesn't. Because children are basically kind and fair minded, they will want to make it easier for newcomers to get to know them and their classroom. From this beginning you can plan a series of activities that will lead to a warm welcome for any ELLs and English-speaking students who happen to enroll later on. I don't want to be overly prescriptive about such activities: they should be those that feel right to you and your students.

The only two things that I consider *musts* are setting up a system of guides and the preparation of welcome kits. Guides are the children who will sit next to a newcomer and show him the ropes. You'll select these helpers as you get to know your English-speaking students. The length of time this guide role needs to last depends on how quickly the newcomer catches on to the rituals, routines, and expectations of the classroom. If the initial match of guide or a partner to a newcomer turns out not to be a good one, you can select a new one at any time. Just remember to make this change with consideration for the feelings of all involved.

Emergencies

I haven't covered the issue of emergencies because I can't predict all the strange things related to ELLs that might happen in any classroom. Yet I have been thinking of some of the unfortunate situations I have witnessed in the past. Occasionally, a child has entered school without the proper clothing to keep her warm or safe. More often, a family cannot afford to buy the required school supplies or cannot find anyone to help them decipher the information in the welcome kit. Sometimes, a young child cries and cannot be consoled. Children may come with head lice, skin diseases, or other contagious conditions that exclude them from being in school until they are medically treated. In all of these situations, you must act—with the aid and consent of your principal—to contact local health or charitable agencies that have the knowledge and means to help these children and get them ready for school.

Details Not Yet Covered

I have left the details of the roles of student guides and the orientation of ELL students for the next chapter, where they seem to fit better. Imagine now that you, your classroom, and your students are as prepared as anyone can be when no one is sure of who is coming or when. Then, let's move on to that exciting day when that first ELL walks through the door and the important days and weeks of learning that follow.

Some Graphic Novels for Intermediate Grades

Queen Bee, by Chynna Clugston
The Baby-Sitters Club series, by Ann M. Martin
Breaking Up: A Fashion High Graphic Novel, by Aimee Friedman

Bone #1: Out from Boneville, by Jeff Smith
Bone #2: The Great Cow Race, by Jeff Smith

Graphic Novel Websites

Comic Books for Young Adults: A Guide for Librarians—
    ublib.buffalo.edu/libraries/units/lml/comics/pages/index.html
No Flying, No Tights—www.noflyingnotights.com
Recommended Graphic Novels for Public Libraries—
    my.voyager.net/~sraiteri/graphicnovels.htm

Welcoming ELLs into the Classroom 3

By now most of the preparations are in place for ELLs to make a smooth entrance into your classroom. The welcome kits are ready to go; the desks are grouped for easy placement of new students; and the work and storage places in the room are labeled with pictures as well as words. If some time has passed since the start of the school year, you already know which children you can count on to be guides for newcomers. They need not be the brightest students in the class, but they should be good, steady workers who follow instructions and can explain their work processes to others. In personality, they are empathetic and patient toward others who are having difficulty. They are also confident enough about their own skills not to worry that they will fall behind if they spend time helping someone else.

The Role of ELL Guides

Choose four to six boys and girls to be guides and meet with them before any ELLs arrive to explain their role. You can always add more guides later on if you need them. Primarily, guides are to be the newcomers' first companions, showing them around, introducing them to other students, and modeling behaviors appropriate in different parts of the school and for all classroom activities. This leading and modeling role will be easier and more comfortable if the guide and the newcomer are the same gender.

Another part of a guide's job is to demonstrate to the newcomer how class work is to be done. She shows her charge where to find textbooks and reference books and how to use them. As she does her own assignments, the guide demonstrates the formalities expected by the teacher, such as where the name and date go on a homework paper, how the paper is numbered or divided, and whether words, sentences, or paragraphs are expected as responses to questions. The ELL's job at this time is to look, listen, and remember how assignments are done. Actually participating and contributing will come soon enough.

The hardest part of being a guide is communicating with a new ELL because a large part of that communication is going to have to be nonverbal. Certainly, guides should talk to their charges. In fact, they should talk as much and as normally as possible, but that doesn't ensure that the newcomers will understand. At times, guides will have to pantomime, demonstrate, or take their charges by the hand and lead them. And sometimes even those efforts will not be enough to enable a newcomer to understand completely. In those instances, a guide may choose to explain again or decide that an ELL's minimal understanding will just have to do for now.

Meeting all these responsibilities is a tall order for any elementary school child. In the lower grades, assigning two guides to alternate time with a newcomer may be the best plan. At any grade level, you should limit a guide's tenure to a week or two so that it does not become burdensome. In a case where a guide and his newcomer turn out to be ill matched, you will have to make a change sooner than that. Most of the time, however, guide-newcomer arrangements work out beautifully, with no excessive strain on anyone.

After the first two weeks, most newcomers will cease to need a guide. They will have made new friends, gotten used to the school and class routines, begun working with academic partners and their table group, and become able to understand and express themselves well enough in English to get along socially.

The Teacher's Role

From the description of the responsibilities of student guides, it may appear that the teacher has very little involvement with entering ELLs. Although that perception is not accurate, the realities of any classroom situation make it very difficult for a teacher to interrupt lessons whenever a newcomer needs help or to give individualized instruction while twenty to thirty other students are waiting to go on with their regular lessons. In order to balance a mixed-language classroom—which is also bound to be a mixed-ability classroom—you have to apportion your time fairly and with great care. When you plan to meet with small groups or individuals, you have to make sure that the rest of the students are engaged in work they can do without a teacher's help.

Because ELLs need a lot of your personal attention in the early weeks of their presence in class, you should try to arrange for some adult assistance for the rest of the class. You may be able to get an aide assigned to your classroom for a couple of hours a day or to enlist some reliable parent volunteers who will schedule themselves for an hour or two on particular days of the week. If all attempts to get adult help fail, you can appoint student aides who are capable of answering most questions for their English-speaking classmates and going over with them what the class has been instructed to do while the teacher is busy helping ELLs.

To help you see how the arrangement of full-class, small-group, and individual time for ELLs can be worked out, I have constructed a model schedule for a third-grade class (see Figure 3.1). I picked third grade because it is the middle of the elementary-grade sequence, so time allocation adjustments for activities in grades both below and above are only minor. Admittedly, this schedule is idealized, with special classes and recesses at the best possible times for children of this age. I realize that most teachers are given more irregular schedules that do not work as well for instruction or breaks. In such cases, you will have to adjust as best you can, but I assure you that it is all right to interrupt the morning or afternoon blocks and resume them after a special class or a recess.

English-Only Teachers in Mixed-Language Classrooms

Figure 3.1   Grade 3 daily schedule

Third-Grade Daily Schedule

8:30–9:00	Morning routines
9:00–10:30	Morning literacy block
	three reading group meetings or reading workshop
10:30–10:45	Recess
10:45–11:45	Literacy block (continued) or special subject (e.g., physical education, music, library)
	one reading group and ELL meeting
11:45–12:30	Lunch and noon recess
12:30–1:30	Math, science, social studies or special subject (e.g., PE, music, library)
1:30–1:45	Afternoon recess
1:45–2:45	Afternoon literacy block, science or social studies
	writing workshop, content-area instruction, projects, or individual help
2:45–3:15	Cleanup, class meeting, recap of day

In a worst-case scenario, even this schedule may not allow enough time for you to take care of all students' individual needs. If so, you will probably do what teachers have always done: give up a part of your lunch period, break, or planning time to help students in need.

Greeting a Newcomer

When the day comes that the first ELL walks through the classroom door, he should be greeted warmly by the teacher and the class, but without any undue fanfare that might be embarrassing. The newcomer should be given one of the seats left open at a table grouping, with his student guide seated next to him. The guide should make sure that the newcomer has a pencil and paper and whatever other supplies the class is using at the time. The guide should also share his own books for rest of the day. Once the new student is settled, which should take only a few minutes, the schedule of class activities for the day should go on as usual.

Probably the first opportunity the guide will have to get acquainted with the new ELL will be morning recess. Let the guide take him out to the playground at recess and try to engage him in a game others are playing. At lunchtime, have hot lunches brought to the classroom so that the three of you can eat and talk. Lunch meetings are the best times for you to make an informal estimate of the amount of English the ELL knows, figure out what his immediate needs are, and present him with the welcome kit. Show him the contents of the kit without trying to explain everything at once. Indicate through a combination of language and pantomime which part of the kit is his for use at school and which part he should take home to his parents. You should take time to go over the necessity card of major places and objects in the school. It is important that he understands what each picture represents and how to use the card to get what he needs from you and other students. He does not have to be able to say the word; if he points to a picture, everyone will know what he wants. Let him know that the student guide will be his helper and reference point for the time being. He should watch what the guide does and where he goes, follow his lead, and ask for his help when he needs it.

This brief orientation is enough for now. Besides, it is all that you can prepare for without knowing the particular ELL. A lot of responsibility falls upon the shoulders of the guide, so choose him carefully, and be ready to spend time with him before and after school and during breaks to hear about any problems he has and to help solve them.

If possible, you should continue lunch meetings over the next few days. You'll need more time to go over parts of the welcome kit that you have not yet explained and to gather as much information as possible about the ELL's language, previous school experience, and family situation. In addition, you may realize that you will have to go outside the school to find help for any emergency problems like the ones mentioned in the last chapter.

As the newcomer learns English words incidentally through interaction with other children over the first week or two, he may begin to say those words and even put them into sentencelike structures, such as "Where pencils?" During the first week, don't be concerned about

English-Only Teachers in Mixed-Language Classrooms

direct teaching of any English vocabulary beyond what is on the card from the welcome kit. The newcomer will pick up words from other students as he needs them. The time for teaching content vocabulary and sentence structure will soon arrive. Now, it is best to let him acclimate himself to the environment, follow his guide, and imitate what the other students say and do.

Welcoming the ELL as a Unique Person

It is not uncommon for students entering a new school to be quiet and appear shy. This behavior is even more common among ELLs newly arrived in the United States, to whom everything looks and sounds strange. They may not ask any questions and may nod at everything you say or show them, indicating that they understand. However, these apparent signs of understanding can actually mean that they are overwhelmed for the moment and want the interaction to end. That is why I suggest that the welcome time be friendly and undemanding and the orientation gradual.

It follows that the noon-hour meetings over the first few days should not be all business. There needs to be time for personal chats about a newcomer's family, where she came from, what she likes to do, and similar information about you and her guide. If communicating verbally is difficult, draw pictures and use pantomime. These devices may not communicate accurately, but they will be a pleasant interchange, and that is good.

At one of the lunch meetings you and the guide should try to learn to say and write a few words or phrases from the newcomer's language, and later introduce them to the class. Greetings are good, as are expressions of politeness, such as "Excuse me" and "Thank you." Post these words on a chart prominently in the classroom and have the class practice pronouncing them under the direction of the newcomer until the children do well enough to satisfy her.

What I am trying to emphasize is that part of any orientation process should be directed toward the teacher and the class. You and your English-speaking students have a lot to learn, and with each new ELL there will be more and different information to assimilate. Technically, learning this information adds to the weight of the classroom curriculum, but in reality it enriches the curriculum and brings it to life, making what appears in textbooks real and relevant.

Gradually, ELL orientation should evolve into individual or small-group instruction in English and participation in whole-class activities. The next chapter describes the process for making these things happen.

Beginning English Instruction

4

As the first week passes, things are likely to be quiet and uneventful. The student guide is doing his job of modeling and explaining, and the ELL newcomer is following his lead, somewhat subdued by all the new routines, new people, and new language he has encountered so quickly. During this time you have met with the newcomer and his guide informally two or three times. You have learned quite a bit about him as a person and a student and have roughly calculated his academic background and knowledge of English. At this point, for teaching purposes, you will want to decide what level ELL he is—1, 2, or 3. I am suggesting fewer and less-technical levels than those ESL teachers use because, as a classroom teacher, you have neither the tools to do a thorough formal assessment nor the capacity to implement a full course of ESL instruction. These three levels and their implications for teaching are described in the chart in Figure 4.1.

Effects of Personal Characteristics on Learning

One thing you will notice after as little as a week is that no matter what the level of competence, there are two types of newcomers. The more

Figure 4.1 Chart of ELL levels

ELL Levels[1]

Characteristics of Level 1 ELLs

Newly arrived in the United States

Speak little or no English

Have moved from place to place and school to school at least once since arriving in the
United States

Have had irregular schooling or no schooling in their own country

Read poorly in their native language; not at all in English

Mostly compliant in school, but not motivated to learn English or other academic subjects

Parents have had little education and speak no English

Family watches native language TV and listens to native language radio

Live in an ethnic community where adults and peers speak the same native language at
home and on the streets

Choose friends only from own ethnic group

Characteristics of Level 2 ELLs

Have lived in the United States for about a year

Can communicate in basic English when necessary

Know many English social expressions

Have had some regular schooling in native country, but were not good students

Can read in their own language, but below grade level

Can decode English text, but with little comprehension

Appreciate the economic benefits of learning English

Parents have had at least an elementary school education

Parents speak some English on the job or in their community

Parents read newspapers in their native language

Live in a mixed ethnic community where several languages are spoken

Listen to American music and go to American movies

Choose to be with native language peers most of the time

1. Students who show four or more of the characteristics listed for a particular level will probably operate at that level in your classroom.

Figure 4.1 *Continued*

Characteristics of Level 3 ELLs

Have lived in the United States for more than a year
Make efforts to communicate in correct English at school and in mixed social situations
Went to school regularly in their native country and in previous places in the United States
Can read materials in native language with at least literal understanding
Were average to good students in previous schools
Can read grade-level material in English with basic comprehension
Parents completed high school or went beyond
There are many books in the home
Parents read newspapers and watch TV shows in English
Live in mixed ethnic community with significant numbers of English-speaking residents
Have both native language and English-speaking friends
Highly motivated to learn English for social, economic, and civic reasons

---

outgoing child has learned several English words and phrases just from being around her English-speaking classmates. As she watched, listened to, and interacted with them, she picked up bits of language and repeated them in conversation. This rapid incidental learning is a product of her self-confidence and strong desire to belong to a group. Although she may not know what all the words she uses mean, she does understand that they are social talk and that using them helps to make her more like her English-speaking classmates.

The second type of newcomer, because of personality or cultural norms, is much quieter. He stays by himself or tags along at the end of a group of boys. He has to be coaxed to join a playground game and, even then, may refuse, saying he doesn't know how to play it. He rarely speaks unless he has to and, then, mostly in single words. Although this second type of child is also learning social language by listening and observing, he will have a harder time than his more outgoing counterpart because he is not practicing what he hears. Nevertheless, both children need some small-group instruction in addition to their incidental learning to broaden their social language and acquire the academic language necessary for grade-level work. Now is the time for you to begin that instruction.

Initial English Instruction

Levels 1 and 2 newcomers will probably need oral language instruction three to five times a week for a month or more before they are ready to participate in regular literacy groups. However, they should meet with these groups right from the beginning for whatever incidental learning they can pick up and to let everyone know that they are included in the class community. Level 3 students will need some support, too, but for a shorter time and on a less regular basis. The best arrangement for ELL language instruction is to have four or five students meet together even if they are at different levels of English competence. But it is also possible for you to do the same type of instruction with a single student if necessary. Since it is important for newcomers to practice what they have been taught, it is also a good idea to have one or two English-speaking students join a language group when you are introducing new material, so they will know how to be learning partners when they are needed. I would not put this added responsibility on those children who are already guides, however. Instead, choose advanced students who usually finish their work early and have the time and temperament to be learning partners.

The kind of initial instruction newcomers need is the introduction of oral vocabulary and sentence structure for everyday living, both inside and outside of school. For the most part, you can teach new words and simple sentences through dramatization and games. By using picture cards, physical demonstrations, objects, and oral language, you can introduce many everyday words, phrases, and common actions. Although I have been saying "you" in the last two paragraphs, I do not mean that the teacher should have to add this extra teaching session to his regular daily schedule. With just a little training, an aide, a parent volunteer, or an older student can lead practice in the activities you have introduced.

Teaching Vocabulary and Sentence Structure

In the beginning, vocabulary and sentence structure activities should be completely oral, but once ELLs have acquired a functional speaking vocabulary, reading and writing words they know can become part of their practice. By varying and combining games, role-playing, and listening to books, you can keep early language learning both interesting and challenging for your students. The following types of activities, listed in order of difficulty, are suitable for levels 1 and 2 students:

> naming picture cards
> playing oral games using vocabulary and sentences
> playing games that include the written forms of words
> role-playing various types of real-life situations using one's self,
>   miniature figures, or hand puppets (also appropriate for level
>   3 students)

Picture Card Games

Unlike the cards in the welcome kit given to ELLs upon their arrival, picture cards for teaching vocabulary are more like flash cards, with objects, creatures, or actions pictured on one side and the written words on the other. Create packs of ten to twenty-five cards that include pictures of everyday living, general academic activities, and categories that students have expressed interest in, such as sports, clothing, or music. If the whole class is studying a particular science or social studies unit at the time, also include some of the most important words from that unit, but not so many that the students will be overwhelmed.

How many cards you present from a pack at any one time depends on the age and language level of the children you are working with, but using the whole pack at once may be too much for level 1 students of any age. On the other hand, since levels 2 and 3 ELLs know the names of most common objects, you could check their knowledge of whole categories and then move them on to academic vocabulary or words from their own special interests.

Vignette 4.1 on page 37 illustrates two games led by an instructional aide. The time frame of these games, which would normally be played over several days or even a few weeks, has been compressed in the vignette in order to give you a more complete picture of the way the games operate.

Oral Language Games, Poems, and Songs

There are also a number of language games that can be played without picture cards that emphasize various useful sentence structures and give continuing practice with newly learned vocabulary. In one such game, the teacher makes a statement and then asks a related question of a particular student. That student answers the question with his own statement and then asks the same question of another student. The game continues until all students have made answering statements and asked questions of the next person. When the teacher's turn comes around again, she makes a new statement and asks a different question. Following are some possible statements and questions. These games are easy for ELLs to play because they require only filling in a slot in a repeated sentence with one or two words.

TEACHER: My name is Carol Finch. What is your name?
STUDENT 1: My name is Anatoly Vladim. What is your name?
STUDENT 2: My name is Geovani Franciosa. What is your name?
TEACHER: I like to eat chicken. What do you like to eat?
STUDENT 1: I like to eat ice cream. What do you like to eat?
STUDENT 2: I like to eat burritos. What do you like to eat?
TEACHER: My favorite color is blue. What is your favorite color?
STUDENT 1: My favorite color is red. What is your favorite color?
STUDENT 2: My favorite color is yellow. What is your favorite color?

Another game involves naming objects or people in the classroom as a way to practice vocabulary. The game goes like this:

TEACHER: I am thinking of something blue, white, and red. What
        is it?
STUDENT 1: Is it Olga's dress?
TEACHER: No, it isn't Olga's dress.
STUDENT 2: Is it Salvador's notebook?
TEACHER: No, it isn't Salvador's notebook.
STUDENT 3: Is it the American flag?
TEACHER: Yes, it is the American flag.

English-Only Teachers in Mixed-Language Classrooms

Games

ng four second-grade ELL students d her at a small table, instructional aide c Sossin introduces the first vocabulary ame they will learn to play. Last week she asked these children what kind of words they wanted to learn, and they decided on different kinds of food. So yesterday she brought in a pile of old magazines and had them look through and cut out pictures of foods they liked or that looked appealing. Last night she pasted twenty-three of those pictures on blank cards, discarding a few the children had chosen that showed uncommon foods or foods presented in combination with other foods. Now she lays out ten cards, one at a time, naming each food and then using its name in a sentence. For example: "French fries. I like to eat french fries." The children repeat each food name and sentence in chorus. Then Ms. Sossin reviews the words by pointing to a card and repeating its name. Again the children repeat the names.

Now the game begins. Each child is allowed to select one card and try to name it. Those who name a food correctly may keep the card. If a child misses, the next child gets a turn. They continue till all ten cards have been claimed. If Ms. Sossin sees that the children are having trouble remembering the names of the foods, she stops the game and reviews again. Finally all cards are named, and the game is played again, but this time children must choose a different card than the one they chose before.

Depending on the facility of the children in naming foods, Ms. Sossin may add more cards to those on the table the second time the game is played or stay with the original ten. In any case, she will add more cards tomorrow and the next day until the children can name all twenty-three cards with ease.

After playing the game over several days, the children have learned to say the names of all the foods in the pack of cards. At this point, Ms. Sossin brings out a second pack on which she has duplicated the pictures and, in addition, printed the names of the foods on the backs. As she lays out about ten of the first set of picture cards again, she shows the duplicate cards and the printed words on the back. She places a picture card and its corresponding word card side by side. The children practice by saying the names of the foods and reading their spellings. After some practice Ms. Sossin moves all the cards around, separating each picture from its written name. The point of this game is to match words with pictures. After a child chooses two cards that she thinks match, she says the word pictured and written and then turns the word card over to see if the pictures really do match. If they do, the player may keep the two cards; if not, she must put them back on the table. When all the cards have been matched, the game is over. The children

continued

then play again so that they can try to match different foods to their written forms. As in the first game, Ms. Sossin gradually adds more picture and word cards to the array on the table until all the cards in the pack are out. She and the children play the game together for a few days, but finally the children are competent enough that they can borrow the packs of cards when they have time and play the game by themselves.

As time goes on, these two games are repeated with new packs of cards covering different categories, chosen by the children or their teacher. Soon, the ELL students grow adept enough to play these games with new words led by a parent volunteer or an older student helper.

The student who answered correctly now takes her turn at describing an object in the room and calling on others to guess what it is.

With a little imagination you can invent similar games that fit the interests and capabilities of your students. The important thing in the early stages of learning English is to give students sentence patterns they can repeat or vary slightly and can fill in with the words they have already learned.

Levels 1 and 2 students should practice games with their learning partners in school or with their family at home every day. Once they have begun to read and write in English, they can play the games silently by writing questions and answers rather than saying them aloud.

In addition to the special games devised for ELLs, there are many whole-class word games, poems, and songs that all children can enjoy. At the primary level, children can play I Spy and Simon Sez. Older students like Twenty Questions, Hangman, and Alphabet Soup.[2] Children of any age like reciting or singing almost any limerick, humorous rhyme, or fun song. Vignette 4.2 on page 39 describes a kindergarten class of mostly ELLs playing and singing "Itsy Bitsy Spider."

---

2. Although called by different names, this game involves having children name an object in a category (e.g., animals, clothes) that starts with a particular letter of the alphabet. The players sit in a circle and clap three or four times to mark the time limit a player has for naming an object.

Vignette 4.2

Kindergartners Learn New Words Through Song

Kindergarten teacher Sue Feder* has taught her class the song "Itsy Bitsy Spider" and the motions that go with it. All of the children, including her ELLs, know it by heart and understand its story. Before introducing the song, Ms. Feder drew and painted a large paper representation of a house and taped it to the classroom wall. She added a three-dimensional drainpipe to the side of the house with a large spider crawling up the outside of it. Now, as the children sing, she moves the spider up and down the waterspout while pointing to the raindrops or the sun above the house. Next, she selects children to do the demonstration while the class sings the song again.

Since the children are thoroughly familiar with the song, Ms. Feder is ready to introduce variations using other parts of the house included in the picture: a roof, a door, and two windows. Around the house are grass, flowers, a tree, drops of rain on one side, and a sun on the other that can also be used in the song.

Each object, except for the sun and the raindrops, is labeled with a three-syllable name (e.g., window frame, wooden door, flower stem, tiled roof, fresh green grass, apple tree) so that its name will fit into the rhythm of the song. Thus, Ms. Feder can begin a variation by singing, "The itsy bitsy spider went up the window frame," and end it with "So, the itsy bitsy spider went up the frame again," keeping the rest of the song in its original form. She will explain the labels and lead the class in using each one in a variation. Finally, she will ask children to volunteer to lead the song, choosing their own variation and pointing to the object being substituted.

Later, after the children have been singing the song and its variations for about a week, Ms. Feder introduces a new variation. She encourages children to suggest new objects and places inside or outside the house to put into the song. The only limitation is that they have to have "three sound parts." Ms. Feder stands ready to help children whose choices have only one or two syllables. When it is Jose's turn, he proudly chooses *outside steps* and shows where they would be on the house picture. The class then sings, "The itsy bitsy spider went up the outside steps," and so on. Betsy follows with *inside steps*, Tomas chooses *kitchen wall*, and, finally, Maria selects *table leg*.

Ms. Feder feels that her experiment has worked out so well for teaching ordinary vocabulary and syllabication that she should look for another song that would so easily yield variations.

---

*This vignette is a composite of a practice observed in several classrooms. The teacher's name is fictitious.

Fortunately, all the while you are teaching vocabulary and sentence structure, your ELL students will continue to learn informally simply by being part of the class. Thus, they are likely to bring new words and sentences into the group sessions that you never thought of. That is why it is important for you to work on creating a place for these students in the classroom community from the moment they come through the door, and why you must continue giving attention to their need for peer acceptance by creating daily situations where all students work and play together.

Role-Playing

In time, picture cards and the games that go with them will grow stale, as ELLs acquire a functional oral vocabulary and gain knowledge of how to read and write the words they can say. When you feel that some games have run their course, it is time to introduce role-playing. Again, this activity works best with a group of students, but it can work even with you and only one student taking the roles. One way to role-play is with small replicas of people, animals, or vehicles. Children often find it less stressful to put words into the mouths of such surrogates than to speak as themselves. In addition, the advantage of using miniature figures is that they can be made to enact a greater range of imaginary situations than the students themselves can. They can fly, run races, fall down, and embrace. Moreover, if you have miniature cars, buses, boats, planes, and so on, you can talk about their parts and what they do. If you have toy animals, you can talk about their names, the names of their young, their food, and where they live.

Using hand puppets or yourselves as characters is somewhat different. The situations tend to be realistic, and you speak only dialogue. With a level 1 student, you might begin with a quite predictable situation, such as a family meal, at which each of you asks for certain foods to be passed, says thank you, and remarks on how good the food tastes. Using toy dishes and flatware adds to the illusion of reality. A level 2 student may be able to start with other types of everyday situations that have a broader range of dialogue possibilities, such as a conversation between a customer and a store clerk, a chat between two friends meeting on the street, or a child asking parental permission to go somewhere or do something special. These dialogues can be spontaneous or planned, rehearsed, and played for an audience.

As part of the reading instruction described in the next chapter, you can also use role-playing to have students retell a story they have read.

Continuing Language Group Meetings

Even after your ELLs have demonstrated their ability to work and learn with the whole class in the content areas, it is a good idea to continue meeting with them in a small-group setting from time to time. How often these meetings should be and their content are matters you must decide based on how well they are doing with the grade-level curriculum and their social relationships. But whether or not everyone is making good progress, you will still want to change the types of activities carried on in their small groups. For ELL students at any level, picture card identification and games may no longer be appealing, even with new categories of words, but role-playing is always motivating and instructionally valuable. Just make the situations different and more challenging in terms of their language demands, and give your students more opportunities to suggest the situations they are most interested in dramatizing. Small-group meetings are also the place to talk over any problems or concerns students might be having academically or socially and to suggest solutions.

Integrating ELLs into Regular Class Activities

Although I've said very little so far about ELLs working with the rest of their class, I have implied that some of that should be going on right from the beginning for students at all levels. In Chapter 7, I describe several strategies that teachers can use to make content subjects manageable for ELLs while enriching the learning of the rest of the class. Whether ELLs get a little or a lot from whole-class instructional experiences, they will still be better off than if they had been isolated until they mastered someone else's idea of an acceptable level of academic English. As long as your whole-class teaching explains new vocabulary, illustrates concepts, and makes complicated issues clear, ELLs and English-speaking students alike will learn effectively.

Before I discuss content learning, however, I want to examine some strategies for teaching reading and writing to ELLs at different levels and for involving them in partner work and group projects. These are complex processes, though not necessarily additional burdens for a busy teacher. In the next chapter I discuss ways of blending ELLs into your regular reading and writing programs.

Teaching Reading and Writing

5

The question that causes the most anxiety for English-only teachers in mixed-language classrooms is "How should I teach reading and writing to my ELLs, when their English skills and knowledge are so far behind those of my English-speaking students?"

Fortunately, the answer is reassuring. You teach them just as you do English-speaking students—allowing them to zoom ahead on their own when they can and giving them varying kinds and amounts of support when they are struggling. As you might expect, primary-grade teachers have the easiest job, not only because most of their native English speakers are also beginning readers and writers but also because young children have a greater aptitude than their older counterparts for learning a second—or third—language and for moving easily between languages.

Most teaching and learning problems arise when ELLs enter American classrooms at fourth grade or later. That is when their knowledge of English vocabulary and grammatical structure is inadequate for comprehending grade-level material. If those students have had little schooling in their own countries, their difficulties are even greater because they also lack the content knowledge their classmates have acquired over their past years in school. Nevertheless, your ELLs can participate in your regular reading program and function satisfactorily in it as long as you provide them with the support they need to understand the material they read, to retain the knowledge and skills they are taught, and to demonstrate what they have learned. This chapter is devoted to teaching strategies that will enable your ELLs to do all of these things.

Reading Methodologies

As I said in the guidelines for teaching in Chapter 1, a whole language approach is the best way to teach ELLs because they need an emphasis on the meaning of texts much more than they need correct pronunciation of words or fluency. In skills-based classrooms, too many ELLs learn to read aloud smoothly without understanding—or even realizing that they ought to understand—what they are reading. Because many foreign languages are more phonetically consistent than English, ELLs who can read in their native language often take to English phonics readily and assume that pronouncing words correctly is all they need to do for the time being. They think that comprehension will come automatically when they learn more oral vocabulary and sentence structures. Unfortunately, many of their teachers think the same way. They do not know that comprehending written texts takes particular kinds of knowledge and ways of thinking that go far beyond decoding skill.

Extra Support in Reading

Whether you use a group structure or a workshop structure to teach reading, your ELLs will need extra support to fully participate in the program and make satisfactory progress. Personally, I prefer to have groups that are reading and discussing the same book. I believe that an interactive group structure automatically provides support to each individual in it through the contributions of all its members. It also encourages lots of oral practice of vocabulary through group discus-

English-Only Teachers in Mixed-Language Classrooms

sion of texts. But if you choose the workshop structure instead, you will have to arrange for reading buddies for your ELLs and provide them with more individual attention than you ordinarily give, so that they, too, can have human interaction about the materials they are reading. Fortunately, however, it is still possible to combine both structures if you use class time efficiently. Even with groups meeting regularly, there are many gaps in the daily schedule when students can read books of their own choosing and confer with the teacher or classmates, as they would in a reading workshop.

Whatever organizational scheme you decide on, ELLs at any grade level are going to need five kinds of support to become successful readers in English:

1. materials that are appropriate

2. the introduction of background information and vocabulary before reading a book or a story

3. an overview of the specific material to be read

4. comprehension assistance during reading

5. opportunities to review material after the initial reading

Although your English-speaking readers need less of these types of support, many of them can also benefit from participating in the activities that I suggest for ELLs.

Since each of the five kinds of support can be provided in different ways, I will describe some of the strategies effective teachers have used, all of which can be increased, decreased, or varied to fit the needs of students and your own teaching style.

Using Appropriate Reading Materials

Don't assume that materials that use phonetically consistent words and short sentences are right for level 1 or 2 ELLs or your struggling English-speaking readers. What writers almost always sacrifice in producing such materials are age appropriateness; interesting, well-constructed stories; and natural language. In the beginning, children may like the fact that they can pronounce the words in such books, but they will soon grow bored with their silly stories and childish language.

At the same time, you should be wary of old children's classics and science fiction for primary-grade ELLs. Even when these books have been shortened and simplified for easier reading, their times, places, plots, and language are still too far removed from the experiences of these children. Both ELLs and struggling English-speaking readers have too little familiarity with the genres of English literature, their forms, and their devices. Instead, these children should be reading modern fiction they can relate to their own lives, homes, and environments, and amply illustrated nonfiction on interesting topics. In addition to the many well-written and well-illustrated trade books on the market today, you should include magazines, comic books, and graphic novels in your reading program for these inexperienced readers. In fact, these materials may be the best ones to start with, since all of them have less written text than a typical book. You should also bring lots of songs and poems into your program because their rhythm, rhyme, and repetition are very appealing to children of all ages and are easier to read than narrative prose. Even long, unfamiliar words in a song or poem seem to be easy for ELLs and struggling readers because they are fun to say and hear. Vignette 5.1 on page 47 illustrates the power of song to make difficult material comprehensible to young children.

Providing Background Before Reading

Teaching thematic units is an easy and efficient way to strengthen background knowledge for all readers. The information and vocabulary you present before students read anything helps to make the books and stories in the unit more understandable. In addition, each thematic piece students read adds more background knowledge and vocabulary, making the next piece easier to read.

You can present background information orally, with photos, drawings, diagrams, and maps; by reading an introductory piece aloud, or by showing real objects from a time or a place. How much background children need depends, of course, on how familiar they are with the genre and content of the material they will be expected to read. If, for example, a book is about life in a foreign country, exotic animals, or fables, you may have to give a lot of background beforehand. If the material is about places and people children are familiar with, you should have to give very little background, and that background is most likely to be vocabulary, such as the names of historical

English-Only Teachers in Mixed-Language Classrooms

Vignette 5.1

Using a Song to Teach Reading

Erin Palmer has chosen an easy, predictable book, *Here We Go Round the Mulberry Bush*, for her lowest second-grade reading group, in which three of the four members are English language learners. Because the book has repeated phrases throughout and pictures on each page that illustrate the action, she expects them to have no trouble reading it. But they do. Even though the children can decode or recognize on sight most of the words, two of them—one an ELL student and the other a native English speaker— read the first page haltingly, as if the book were in some strange language. The word *mulberry* in the first line stumps all the children; they cannot recognize it or sound it out. With the teacher's help, Antonio finally pronounces the word, but clearly he does not know what it means. Realizing that the word is unfamiliar to all the children, Ms. Palmer explains that a mulberry bush is a type of low-growing plant with some kind of fruit on it. She can go no further because she is not sure she has ever seen one herself, and the illustration on the page shows just a bare-branched tree. So she tells the group that this book is really a singing game that children used to play when she was young. Then she sings the first verse for them, which, except for a few different words,[1] is exactly what appears on the book's first page.

The children's faces light up. Now they get it. The language seemed strange to them because they did not know it was a song and they were not familiar with old-fashioned terms like *round* for *around*. After hearing his teacher sing the song only once, Antonio breezes through the first page, almost singing, and reading the few words that are different in print from the song correctly. The other children also go swiftly and smoothly through the rest of the book, helped by the illustrations that show children brushing their teeth, combing their hair, and getting dressed for school. Finally, the group sings the whole book together.

Because things are now going so smoothly, Ms. Palmer decides to extend this reading lesson into a vocabulary lesson. She asks the children if they can think of other things they do before going to school in the morning that will fit into the song. Sada suggests, "This is the way we eat our cereal," and the children sing and pantomime it. Each child suggests something new, and again, they all sing and pantomime the action. After a few minutes more, Ms. Palmer dismisses the group and the children go back to their seats, humming their new song.

As Ms. Palmer sits alone before calling her next reading group, she realizes that she has learned two important lessons from this experience: (1) the children faltered at first because they did not realize they were reading a song, one that did not follow the normal patterns of narrative or conversation; and (2) the rhythm, repetition, and melody, along with the illustrations, served as scaffolds for the children to master the reading of unfamiliar words. She determines to use more songs and poems with these children who are struggling with both spoken English and reading.

---

1. The song, as Ms. Palmer remembers it, has the words "early in the morning," while the words in the book are "on a cold and frosty morning."

characters or indigenous plants. Remember, though, that in any type of background presentation, children need opportunities to ask questions, study visual exhibits carefully, and examine objects closely.

Other sources of background information are picture books, videos, student books made by previous classes, and computer CDs. These materials engage children easily and require little teacher assistance or supervision. However, you should try to match students with particular materials suited to the background knowledge they already have.

Providing an Overview

Even when students are given material to read on a familiar topic that is within their capabilities, it helps if they get an overview beforehand, so they have an idea of the purpose, content, and flow of the material. An overview is more important in a school setting than it is when children are reading on their own at home because the school reading time each day is limited by the schedule of subjects and interrupted by all the other things going on in the classroom and the school. At school, children rarely get to read a whole story or chapter in one sitting, or even to stop reading at a natural breaking point in the narrative. All readers want reading a book to be a coherent experience, not a series of arbitrarily sized chunks separated by another subject, a weekend, or a fire drill. An overview gives readers a plan or a pattern they can hang onto when their reading is being interrupted more than once every day.

With young children, a picture walk through a book can be enough of an overview since primary-level books introduce the characters and portray most of the story action through pictures. After a picture walk, it may be a good idea for the group to make an outline chart of the story with both words and pictures. This chart will help hold the story overview in children's memories and allow them to correct any misconceptions as they actually read it.

For older students, whose books have few, if any, illustrations, the teacher can present an overview by telling the group what the story is about, reading a few pages aloud at the beginning, and, as she reads, voicing her own predictions about where the plot is going. At the same time she can encourage students to share their own thinking about what might be ahead. As the students proceed with their reading, they can also benefit from creating a plot outline chart. With a long or com-

English-Only Teachers in Mixed-Language Classrooms

plicated book, the teacher can sustain students' interest and under-standing by regularly reviewing the most recent parts of the chart and asking students to add some details they've gleaned from further reading or to correct misunderstandings. She can also reengage students in each new chapter or section by reading a few intriguing paragraphs aloud before asking them to go on with their own reading.

For experienced readers, group talking, wondering, and predicting at the beginning of a book provide a lot of information: what the main characters are like, the setting, the tone, the genre of the book, and the direction of the plot. Remember that according to literary experts, there are only twelve plots in all of fiction, and experienced readers—even young ones—subconsciously know those plots and use that knowledge to read new books. For example, one common plot in books for young children is that of three siblings and three tasks, with the youngest (or smartest, or most virtuous) being the one who succeeds. We see this plot in *The Three Billy Goats Gruff*, *The Three Little Pigs*, and *Cinderella*. There are variations in *Goldilocks and the Three Bears* and *Rumplestiltskin* and in adult literature such as *King Lear* and *Sir Gawain and the Green Knight*.

As an adolescent, I developed the habit of approaching a new book by reading the first and the last chapters and then deciding if I wanted to read the rest of it. This habit, which has stayed with me throughout my adult life, doesn't spoil a story for me. Instead it allows me to know what kind of book I have in hand and whether or not I want to find out the details of the plot and get to know the characters better. For me, reading fiction is kind of like putting together the perimeter of a jigsaw puzzle and then filling in the middle. Although I don't advocate this practice for everyone, I think there's some logic to it. It gives the reader a sense of the book as a whole and allows him to enjoy each chapter for itself and fit it into the pattern of the book. Of course, I realize that many readers like the suspense and tension that go with not knowing what will happen next, so my way of reading is not for them.

The introductory strategies I have just described work quite well for levels 2 and 3 ELLs who come with the ability to understand the material they are asked to read at a literal level and who have some knowledge of genres and literary devices in their own language. But if a teacher has students who are newcomers to written English and schooling, even more support may be necessary. One possibility is to have an English-speaking student audio record each chapter the day before the whole reading group will discuss it. A level 1 ELL can listen to the recording and follow the written version in the book by running her finger under each word while others read the chapter silently. If she doesn't understand something, she can also stop the recording and replay a part or ask a classmate for help.

Another strategy that works for ELLs is to have them preread at least part of a chapter with a partner. A third strategy, suitable for levels 1 and 2 students, is to give them a simplified and amply illustrated version of a story to read before going on to the authentic and complete version. One way to ensure that you have such versions on hand is to have students—English-speaking students or ELLs—from previous years construct them after they have read a full version. This is an excellent review activity for those who have read the books and a tremendous support to those who are now going to read them.

For ELLs whose English reading is extremely weak, having a partner to read with is the most helpful strategy because the partner can help them stay on track and can explain any words they don't understand. But any of the strategies described here will better prepare ELLs for group reading and discussion.

Supporting Comprehension

Whether readings are fiction, nonfiction, poetry, technical material, or journalism, teachers can support students' comprehension in a number of ways. These support techniques are especially important for ELLs, who may be concentrating on just pronouncing words or getting the literal meaning of sentences. One powerful technique, which does not seem like instruction at all, is showing students how to think as they read. To set the pattern and encourage it to become a habit, you need to demonstrate this technique continually as you read aloud. Although you don't want to take the pleasure out of a story by overdoing a demonstration of your thinking processes, an occasional question to yourself about the meaning of a word or the significance of a character's action at a natural breaking point in the story can show students that this is what good readers normally do in their heads. You can also stop at the end of an episode and predict what will happen next and then ask your students if they agree or have different ideas about how the story will go. Through these demonstrations you will be gently persuading nonreflective readers that they can get more meaning and pleasure out of a book by continually questioning it and themselves as they read. Vignette 5.2 on page 52 shows how one teacher uses this technique skillfully while reading aloud to her fifth-grade class, more than half of which are ELLs.

Teachers can also help students' comprehension by showing them that story context often defines unfamiliar words. Begin by going over a chapter before a group session and underlining words that your students are not likely to know. Then read on a bit to see if information about their meanings is given in the text. When you meet with the group, you will have to explain those words that are not defined in context, but give your students a chance to make guesses about them first. They may surprise you. With words that are explained in the text, ask them to guess and then read on and guess again. Even though this technique may not always produce accurate definitions, it will allow your students to get closer to meanings through their own sleuthing. Ultimately, this is what good readers do; rarely do they stop in the middle of a good story to look up a word in a dictionary.

When an unfamiliar word is central to the topic being studied or the story being read, be sure to list it on a chart for the unit along with a simple definition. Incidentally, don't use dictionary definitions in this activity. They tend to be far too technical and to include explanations that are just as puzzling as the word being looked up.

The most effective way to both aid and assess comprehension is to have students retell, act out, or write about the events and/or information they have just read. The special benefit of this strategy is that it can be modified for ELLs and English-speaking students of all abilities. From level 1 ELLs, you might ask only for a short sequence of drawings with sentences or key words underneath each one, for a pantomime of the story action with a few spoken words here and there, or for a three-sentence written summary. From levels 2 and 3 ELLs, you might expect a retelling, a more verbal element in a dramatization, or a simplified and illustrated version for future ELLs, as described earlier in this chapter. Your English-speaking students can use any of the three modes suggested to produce a longer, more detailed account of the story that includes some interpretation of characters' motivations and/or personalities.

Another variation that may be more engaging for creatively inclined students than the ways described previously is to have students choose a character and produce a diary entry for each chapter from

Reading Aloud to Fifth Graders

Gathering her fifth-grade class on the rug in one corner of the classroom, Linda Spangler prepares to read aloud from a new book, *The Lion, the Witch and the Wardrobe*, by C. S. Lewis. She knows that this book will be a particularly challenging one for her mostly ELL class because of its fantastic plot, its formal writing style, and the large number of unfamiliar words reflecting English life in the early part of the twentieth century. Yet she has decided to read this book aloud because it has been made into a children's movie that many of her students want to see. Thus, they are motivated to hear the original story, and hearing it will help those who will later see the movie to better understand the plot and characters. Another factor in choosing this book to read aloud is her unspoken determination to bring a variety of high-quality literature to her students, who might not encounter much of it in their everyday lives or select such books from the library on their own. C. S. Lewis, who has written many other children's books (and adult books), is an author that she believes children should become familiar with.

In beginning the book, Ms. Spangler does not describe the book's historical or geographical background, assuming—correctly, I think—that her students want to get right into the story. Her only introduction is to read the author's dedication to his goddaughter, Lucy, and to point out that he has made her one of the major characters in the story.

As she reads the story, Ms. Spangler pauses from time to time to explain unfamiliar words and expressions. Instinctively, it seems, she knows which words will puzzle both her ELLs and her English-speaking students. For example, she chooses to define *wireless* (an old type of radio), *mothballs*, and *wardrobe* (a large piece of furniture in which to store clothing), because they are all unfamiliar terms to today's young people of any culture. Before giving the definitions, however, she asks students to make guesses about these words, and then she moves from the words' modern meanings backward in time to their meanings in the older context of the book. The only vernacular expression she stops to define herself is "We had fallen on our feet," using the example of what cats do to explain the meaning of the idiom still used today.

During the reading of the first chapter, the class appears very engaged. Whether or not they understand every word they hear, they comprehend enough to enjoy the classic story.

After this introduction Ms. Spangler continues reading the book every day for nearly six weeks. As she reads, she still pauses periodically to examine strange words and expressions with her class. At the same time, she is careful not to interrupt the most exciting passages or to make the book seem like schoolwork by stopping too often. Between chapters she takes time for discussion about what is going on in the story, encouraging her students to draw inferences from past chapters and make predictions about what might happen next.

Figure 5.1 Student's diary entry

> *Our wagon train has decided to take the Cheyenne River Trail because we can travel with safety knowing rivers will always be near and no Indians will be around to attack us. There are also forests which means hunting will be good. The Cheyenne River Trail will be longer but over all much safer to travel and will most likely give our whole wagon train much confidence to make the long trip to Oregon without worrying as much as they might be taking another trail.*
>
> *Signed,*
> *Tom Cassin*

the character's point of view. Although you may be tempted to encourage your ELLs to choose minor characters because there is less to say about them, major characters are more interesting to all students. Students pay more attention to what those characters do and say, so it is easier for them to write about them than minor characters. Figure 5.1 is an example of a child's diary entry written while reading fiction about the western movement in the United States.

In working with ELL students of any level, teachers should allow them more leeway in summarizing what they have read than English-speaking students because the ELLs are building vocabulary and sentence structure at the same time as they are demonstrating reading comprehension. To make this difficult task easier for ELLs, you may want to split a retelling between two or three students. And don't hesitate to prompt students who are struggling with retelling by asking questions that include one or more of the words they are groping for or by supplying a sentence or two when they seem to have run dry. Always let ELL students know that it is all right to fill in the gaps in a retelling, dramatization, or written piece with words or sentences from their native language. Although you may not completely understand what they have substituted, the fact that students are saying something that has meaning for them indicates understanding.

Reviewing and Rereading

All children benefit from reviewing material they have read in their reading groups or in reading workshop, but especially ELLs, who may have had to concentrate so hard on the mechanics of reading the first time through that they did not fully enjoy the story. Their comprehension also improves when they can read a story a second time at their own speed and without interruptions. Specifically, through rereading, ELLs strengthen their recall of facts, become more familiar with new vocabulary, and increase their understanding of the author's message. In the process they may also make large strides in fluency.

ELLs can review a book or a chapter they have studied by reading it to a partner in school or a family member at home. They can also tape-record their oral reading and listen to it afterward to assess their own fluency and pronunciation. Another possibility is to have them read to adult volunteers or visitors. In one classroom I visited, a grandfather of one of the children came to school once a week just to have students read stories to him. To earn this privilege, students had to practice rereading a story until they could read it correctly and fluently with expression.

Finally, students can review a story they have studied for the purposes of writing, retelling, or dramatizing it, or they can go over a primary-level book they enjoyed in the past as preparation for reading it aloud to younger children in another classroom. These kinds of reviewing are not just practice to please the teacher, which some students may find boring and pointless, but purposeful preparation for self-enhancing performances.

To illustrate some of the supportive reading strategies I have described, I offer a vignette of a grades 1 and 2 class, with more than 70

English-Only Teachers in Mixed-Language Classrooms

percent ELLs in it, who were using such strategies independently and in groups during their reading block (see Vignette 5.3 on page 56).

The Benefits of Reading Aloud

Although I have advocated teachers reading aloud to students, I did not list it as a separate support strategy for ELLs because I believe it should be an essential component of the overall curriculum for all students. In the first place, when a teacher reads aloud, he introduces students to types of literature, authors, and specific books they might never stumble upon on their own. He also introduces them to times, places, and kinds of people they have not yet—and may never—meet in their ordinary lives. In addition, hearing books read aloud increases children's vocabularies and familiarizes them with the literary genres, forms, and devices that they will meet over and over again in their own reading. These benefits accrue even when children have heard a book before. The most important point to remember is that learning gained through listening to books read aloud transfers to new reading. Every book a child hears makes the next book she reads easier to comprehend and the child a more eclectic and discerning reader.

Earlier I mentioned that experts have identified only twelve literary plots, which have been repeated over the ages, with varied details, in different pieces of literature. Literary forms, devices, and conventions used by writers of fiction, nonfiction, and poetry, while not nearly as limited in number as plotlines, appear over and over in everything we read. Think about the fairy tale language conventions of "once upon a time" and "they lived happily ever after," or the familiar literary forms of the whodunit and the limerick. Consider authors' use of flashbacks and the all-knowing narrator, impossibilities in real life that are commonly used devices in realistic fiction.

In journalism we see the universal form of headline and sub-headline, meant to attract our interest and arouse our curiosity, followed by the introductory paragraph that briefly tells us who did what, where, and when. Then, the paragraphs that give us the details follow, often in story form, providing the human-interest part of the article. As for conventions in journalism, think about how articles give us the ages of people and call them by their full names the first time they are

Vignette 5.3

Reading Activities in a Primary Classroom

The thematic literature unit for the current month in Emma Harris' grades 1 and 2 classroom is Animals Everywhere. Ms. Harris has collected a large array of books and background materials about animals in all parts of the world, some fiction but most nonfiction. During the morning reading block she works with one group at a time on a shared reading while the other children work independently or in small groups with an aide or a volunteer. Because more than 70 percent of her students are ELLs, she has grouped children by both reading ability and English language competence.

In the first group to meet this morning there are four ELLs and one English-speaking child. Among the books they have read are *Animals Do the Strangest Things*, by Leonora and Arthur Hornblow, *Amazing Eggs*, by Clare Llewellyn, and *Teeth*, by Greg Pyers. Their task today is to write questions and answers based on the information they have learned from these books in preparation for running a quiz game among their classmates. They pore over the books they have read to find interesting and important questions and then check to make sure they have the right answers. After the children have finished their individual work, they share their questions and answers with each other to make sure they are clear and correct.

While the question writing is going on, the rest of the class is involved in other kinds of work on the same animal theme. Most of the children are reading different books at their seats, either silently to themselves or softly with a partner. A few children are gathered around a computer, watching an animal story on a CD. Although the story is fiction, its main purpose is to give the children information about the lives of animals.

One small group, whose English writing skills are minimal, are working with an adult volunteer to draw pictures of animals they have read about. Each child must draw two animals from the mountains and two from the desert and then write a one-sentence caption for each picture that gives some information about the animal portrayed. When it is this group's turn to meet with Ms. Harris, they will explain their drawings and read their captions. Then they will begin to read a new book, *Baby Elephant Gets Lost*, by Sandra Iverson.

Within the next few days, the group who is writing questions will hold a quiz game for their classmates. They will tell the others in advance which books the questions come from and will invite them to read them if they have not yet done so. Those children who want to participate in the quiz will answer questions orally without the opportunity to look up information at the last minute.

The reading group that is writing the questions will act as quizmasters, stationing themselves at a large table placed prominently in the classroom. They will call on the contestants, ask the questions, and decide on the correctness of the answers. Children who are not involved in the quiz will serve as the audience, cheering on the contestants.

mentioned (without Mr., Mrs., etc.) and from then on by their last names only. Again, familiarity with these forms and devices that readers build through continued exposure supports their comprehension.

Supporting ELLs' Writing

The importance of writing in relation to reading has already been described as a support strategy, but there are many other types of writing that should to be regular experiences for all students, especially ELLs. However, there is a problem. Writing is harder than speaking or reading because it involves specific knowledge and a number of cognitive and mechanical skills that students must use simultaneously. In order to write we have to give our attention to form, content, grammatical structure, rhetorical devices, word selection, paragraphing, spelling, handwriting, punctuation, and capitalization. As all teachers know, being in control of all of these components at once is a challenge for native English-speaking students. How much more of a challenge it must be for ELLs, especially those who have had little previous schooling in any language. Although teachers cannot exempt ELLs from the multiple demands of writing, they can use strategies that will make writing a more manageable and pleasurable activity. Because one of our teaching goals is to make clear, persuasive, and satisfying writing a part of all students' lives, we have a special responsibility to enable ELLs to master its difficulties slowly, steadily, and with understanding.

Without deprecating the importance of personal narratives, essays, and creative fiction as writing experiences all students should have, I must emphasize that there is also a place for imitating the writing of professional writers in any writing program. In other words, students can learn a lot about writing from following good models. I believe that this aspect of learning about writing is especially valuable as a support for ELLs, who have fewer English language resources of their own to rely on than their English-speaking classmates. I am not saying that they don't have fascinating experiences and imaginative stories to tell, only that they have fewer tools with which to convey them effectively in English. One way they can acquire those tools and learn to use them is by working with models, varying them only a little at first, but more and more as time goes on, and finally using them only as the subconscious base for structure, grammatical accuracy, and style.

One popular book I have cited elsewhere as an example of a good model for elementary school students in any grade is *Alexander and the Terrible, Horrible, No Good, Very Bad Day,* by Judith Viorst. Although this book is not a literary masterpiece, it is a story close to the experiences of every child and an exceptionally flexible model for writing. In the original, Alexander, the youngest of three brothers, tells about an ordinary school day on which everything went wrong for him, from having a bad seat in the family car in the morning, to an unappetizing school lunch, to a dentist appointment after school, and finally to having his mother buy him a pair of shoes he didn't like. Not only can children relate to Alexander's run of minor misfortunes, but they can also readily substitute their own, or they can change the whole basic idea of the book to a wonderful day on which everything went right. In Figure 5.2A is an example of a piece written by a grade 3 English-speaking student using the *Alexander* model to describe her own "very good day."

In the following list are a few other books that work well as models for ELL writing. You will note that they are all primary-level books because ELLs in the intermediate grades, or even middle school, need short, uncomplicated plots as models. Not only are most of the more mature books they are able to read too long and without a discernible plot pattern to use as a basis for writing, but their stories cannot be so easily varied to accommodate real-life experiences or imaginative ideas.

> *Q Is for Duck: An Alphabet Guessing Game,* by Mary Elting and Michael Folsom
> *Fortunately,* by Remy Charlip
> *Mary Wore Her Red Dress,* by Merle Peek
> *If You Give a Mouse a Cookie,* by Laura Joffe Numeroff
> *Where the Wild Things Are,* by Maurice Sendak

Models for writing can also come from other sources. One readily available source is well-known fairy tales, fables, and myths. If you decide to use any of these sources, it is a good idea to present different versions so students see that storytellers in the past have often

Figure 5.2A Story based on *Alexander and the Terrible, Horrible, No Good, Very Bad Day*

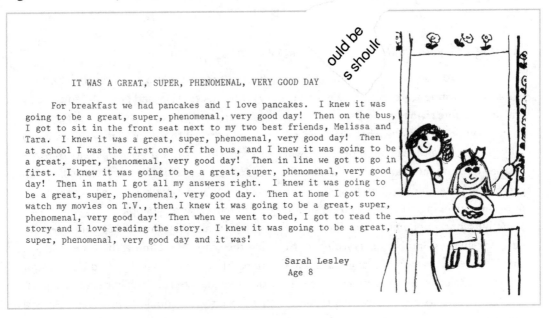

IT WAS A GREAT, SUPER, PHENOMENAL, VERY GOOD DAY

    For breakfast we had pancakes and I love pancakes. I knew it was
going to be a great, super, phenomenal, very good day! Then on the bus,
I got to sit in the front seat next to my two best friends, Melissa and
Tara. I knew it was a great, super, phenomenal, very good day! Then
at school I was the first one off the bus, and I knew it was going to be
a great, super, phenomenal, very good day! Then in line we got to go in
first. I knew it was going to be a great, super, phenomenal, very good
day! Then in math I got all my answers right. I knew it was going to
be a great, super, phenomenal, very good day. Then at home I got to
watch my movies on T.V., then I knew it was going to be a great, super,
phenomenal, very good day! Then when we went to bed, I got to read the
story and I love reading the story. I knew it was going to be a great,
super, phenomenal, very good day and it was!

                                            Sarah Lesley
                                            Age 8

varied the basic plots. Another source is the group stories the class has written under the teacher's guidance. The advantage is that your ELLs participated in the creation of these stories, so they already know the process and they have a personal investment in the form. By writing their own variation on a group story, students get the chance to make all the parts come out the way they want them to instead of having to compromise with their classmates. Vignette 5.4 on page 60 describes how one second-grade class wrote a group fairy tale as preparation for writing their own. Notice that reading and being read to were also part of this class' experience, which helped them to understand the fairy tale genre and use it in their own writing.

    Another type of writing that ELLs at any level can manage is the visual story with written dialogue, mentioned earlier as a way that students can summarize what they've read. In using this concept for both creative writing and personal narratives, you can introduce a format that is much like a beginning reading book, with a small amount of text illustrated by pictures, or one like a comic book, with bubbles for characters' speech. These two possibilities allow children to use narrative and/or dialogue—along with pictures—to tell their stories,

Vignette 5.4

Writing Fairy Tales in a Primary Classroom

Sharla Sanford's second graders have been working on writing a group fairy tale for several days. Before trying to compose their own story, they heard their teacher read several fairy tales aloud and read a few on their own. As they became familiar with the fairy tale genre they were able to identify some of its most prominent ingredients: a hero, a villain, something bad happening, and finally, the hero (or heroes) making everything right again. They also recognized that good characters in fairy tales are often members of royalty and bad characters are usually witches, dragons, sorcerers, or other imaginary creatures with magical powers.

When the students felt ready to begin their own story, Ms. Sanford insisted that they first make a plan of the characters and the plot. Although individual children suggested a number of very different story plans, their teacher deftly led them to consensus. They decided on a king, a queen, and an evil witch. Their plot would involve the kidnapping of the queen and her husband's efforts to get her back. The story would end happily with the queen's return and the witch's punishment.

On the day I visited, the completed parts of the story appeared on five large sheets of chart paper taped to one of the classroom walls. Scratch outs and words written between the lines showed that the children had made changes as they went along. Several sticky notes were also stuck on the charts in various places. They had been placed there by children who'd had questions or suggestions about parts of the story as they were written so far. One of the suggestions was that the characters (e.g., king, queen, witch) be given names to help identify them and make them seem more like real people.

Before allowing the class to continue writing the story, Ms. Sanford had the students reread in chorus what they had done so far and then directed each child to talk to a partner about what should happen next. After a couple of minutes of partner discussion, several children raised their hands to make suggestions. One child suggested that the palace guards should capture the witch and put her in the dungeon. Another thought that the witch should use her magic wand to hold back the guards and escape. A third child said that the king, disguised as a guard, should grab the witch, take her wand from her, and set the queen free.

The general feeling of the class was that the story should go on a while longer, so the witch could not be captured right then. Amalia came up with the following piece of dialogue to continue the story:

> "Ha, ha, ha," laughed the witch. "The queen will never leave my mansion again."

continued

Then Viktor added:

"You'll never take the queen away from me."

Because time was short, the class wrote no more as a group that day. Instead the children went back to their seats and continued working on individual pieces they had started a few days ago. Some of their stories were fairy tales, but others were realistic accounts of children's adventures. While the children wrote or talked about their stories with a partner, Ms. Sanford moved around the room, helping children who were stuck on some aspect of the plot or who were ready to do some editing.

Figure 5.2B   **Sharla Sanford with students working on writing**

working around the problems of unknown words and complex sentence structures. Vignette 5.5 on page 62 describes how one grades 1 and 2 teacher introduced her students to writing comic strips and shows an example of finished work by an ELL. Incidentally, this is the same class described earlier, in Vignette 5.3.

A third type of writing, suitable for ELLs who have not yet learned much vocabulary or grammar, is a variation on the familiar language experience approach to teaching reading. In this instance children

Creating Superhero Comic Strips

Grades 1 and 2 teacher Emma Harris has decided to end the school year with an engaging project on superheroes. Since her class, which includes 70 percent ELLs, already knows a lot about various superheroes through television, films, video games, and comics in their home lives, she feels they need no further background knowledge from her. All she has to do is introduce the topic and they will be ready to plunge into the project.

When the children are gathered on the rug in a corner of the room for the usual introduction to the afternoon's activities, she suggests the project. Each student is to think of himself as a superhero, make up a name, design a costume, decide on his super powers, and choose a special place to change into his costume. The children respond enthusiastically, many of them quickly declaring what kind of hero they'd like to be.

After some conversation, Ms. Harris directs all the children to turn to a neighbor on the rug and talk with her about their ideas for a superhero identity. After about a minute, she stops the conversation and asks if there are any children who are still undecided. If so, they may stay and talk with her while the others go back to their desks and get started. Before anyone is allowed to leave the rug, however, the teacher makes clear the task for today: they are to draw their superhero, name her or him, describe the hero's powers, and draw the special changing place the hero uses. In Figure 5.3, Ms. Harris goes over the elements of a superhero that need to be included in their comic strips.

Figure 5.3   Ms. Harris discusses the elements of a superhero with her class

continued

At the end of the session, children introduce themselves as their super alter ego. They act out their persona and show and tell their new identity. Tomorrow, Ms. Harris tells them, they will draw a comic strip depicting one of their hero's adventures, so they should think about the adventure they want to illustrate.

When the class meets the following day, Ms. Harris shows the comic strip she has been working on. Her hero is Super Teacher, who has the power to look inside children's heads. In the story depicted in the comic strip, Super Teacher notices that her whole class appears to be asleep. She looks inside their heads and, to her surprise, finds them all empty. She goes to her secret hideout in the library and becomes Super Teacher. Realizing that the villain Idea Stealer is on the loose in her classroom, Super Teacher begins to track him down. At this point, Ms. Harris tells the class that she is stuck. She doesn't know how to finish the story. Several children make suggestions, all of them rather clever. The teacher listens carefully, thanks the students for their help, and says she thinks she will be able to finish her comic strip now.

Before sending the children back to their seats to work on their own comic strip stories, Ms. Harris instructs them to talk with a neighbor again. They need to be sure they have a mystery or a problem in their story and a villain who is responsible. The point of the story is to show how the hero defeats the villain and makes everything all right again.

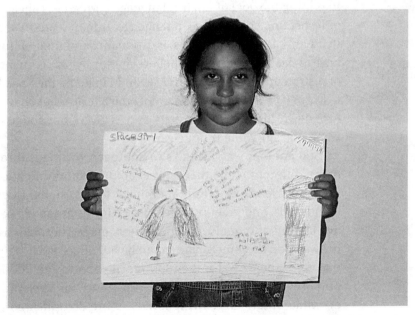

Figure 5.4   Veronica with her superhero, Spacegirl

continued

When I visit the class the next day, several children have created their superheroes and completed their comic strips; others are still working. In Figure 5.4 (on the previous page) you can see a photo of one ELL and the cover page for her comic strip. There were many other clever and well-drawn strips in the classroom, but I chose this one because it was the most legible for reproduction in this book.

To close up the project, the children share their comic strips with their friends (in small groups, show-and-tell style). Finally, Ms. Harris makes photocopies of the comics, so the children can swap with their friends and have a comic collection to take home to read to their families.

dictate their stories to the teacher or a competent peer, who helps them make things clear and complete by asking questions and suggesting changes in sentence structure, on the pragmatic principle of "this is the way we say it in English."

I am aware that what I have just suggested may be controversial. In putting the goal of English language correctness ahead of the goal of respecting children's own language, it may seem to some readers that I am disrespecting ELLs' individuality and their culture. You will have to decide whether you believe my suggestion is an insult to ELLs or a strategy for modeling the second language they need and want to learn. If you feel that you cannot ethically do what I have described, take down the dictation exactly as it is given, but still ask questions where the story line is not clear.

Still another way for ELLs to approach writing is through trying many different short pieces of everyday communication, such as notes to friends or family members, labels, signs, slogans, titles, menus, ads, and greeting cards. These forms are made easier by the availability of models in newspapers, magazines, classrooms, and hallways, on the streets, and in public buildings. Such simple tasks as making nameplates for their lockers, notebooks, and desks can be a purposeful and satisfying writing experience for level 1 ELLs to work on while others are writing longer, more complicated pieces. If a student's handwriting is especially artistic, other students may want him to make nameplates for them, too. Teachers can always find objects and places they want labeled or a bulletin board that needs a heading. They can ask an ELL to make a poster of the school lunch menus for the week or to copy the day's schedule of classes on the chalkboard. At a somewhat more sophisticated level, any classroom would welcome a set of good-looking folded cards that say on the front, "Happy Birthday," or "Congratulations," or "We miss you," which students could use to write personal greetings to friends or family inside. Although a number of the tasks just mentioned are copying rather than original writing, they still have value. All of them are purposeful activities that teach useful vocabulary and the rudiments of spelling, grammar, and cultural conventions. The next steps for ELLs are more original: captions for drawings, short advertisements for school activities or services (e.g., "Buy popcorn in Rm. 17 today."), and notes to their friends. As might be expected, friendly notes are likely to be filled with errors that will never be corrected. Still, these flawed writings teach fluency, build confidence, and encourage students to write longer pieces, write more often, and attempt the academic writing their classmates are doing.

Having observed the several types of writing activities suggested here in elementary classrooms, I believe they not only advance the written competence of ELLs but also take the pressure off the teacher to push students into the usual types of classroom writing that they are not yet ready for. Everything suggested in this chapter has been calculated to balance ELLs' needs with the needs of other students in the classroom and the heavy responsibilities you, as a classroom teacher, already carry. No, they are not the silver bullets we all dream of discovering, but they are practical and effective learning experiences. With everyone working together and using the wisdom born of experience, your classroom can be a place where all students learn, and you are able to practice the art of teaching in its finest form.

Content Learning 6

At any grade level, math, science, history, and geography are harder for ELLs to learn and harder for teachers to teach than reading and writing. Not only do these subjects release a torrent of unfamiliar vocabulary words on students' heads, but they also overwhelm them with a flood of information that seems to have no connection to the lives they lead or the world they know. To make things worse, most subject area textbooks are not reader friendly. In an attempt to include everything any teacher or critic could possibly want, while taking a politically neutral stance, they skim over thousands of facts without plumbing the depths or touching on the human elements of any topic they cover. As a result, ELLs—and also many English-speaking students—are able to read the words in their texts without getting much meaning from them or experiencing any desire to know more.

Fortunately, most of the teachers whose classrooms I visited for this book planned, created, and continuously improved their content-area units, largely without using textbooks, to make them comprehensible for ELLs and still challenging for English-speaking students. I stand in awe of these teachers: I was continually impressed by how rich in content their units were. They had found broader, deeper, and more personal approaches to content teaching, and their students showed more knowledge of content and more enthusiasm for learning than I have seen in a long time. I must also give a great deal of credit to Project GLAD (Guided Language Acquisition Design)[1], in which all these teachers had been trained, for imbuing them with a larger view of what a content unit should be and providing them with a variety of strategies for teaching content to ELLs and all other students.

In this chapter I give a brief overview of GLAD, as I understand it from my own training in the project. But my main focus is on how teachers have adapted what they learned from their GLAD training to the specific needs of their students, the expectations of their schools' curricula, the demands of state testing programs, and their own teaching styles.

The GLAD Project

The GLAD project was developed more than twenty years ago to instruct teachers in the basics of creating a structured English immersion program for ELLs in regular classrooms. GLAD does not offer a curriculum, commercial materials for student use, or a "how to do it" guide for teachers. Its sole "product" is a professional development workshop that explains its philosophical approach to teaching and introduces an array of effective teaching strategies. The first part of the workshop includes an impressive overview of the research that underlies the GLAD philosophy and strategies. A number of visual formats for organizing material, sample units for different grade levels, and patterns for chants and songs that can serve as models for teachers to create their own are also included. In the second part of the workshop, teachers spend five mornings observing a GLAD trainer working with a class of children and five afternoons discussing what they have seen.

Within the limits of this book I am not able to reproduce the set of principles or describe the full array of strategies taught in a GLAD

---

1. GLAD was created by Marcia Brechtel and her teaching partner, Linnea Haley, in Fountain Valley, California. In 1991 the U.S. Department of Education declared it a Project of Academic Excellence, and it was cited as an "exemplary" program by the California Department of Education. Marcia Brechtel continues to train local trainers as director of training for Project GLAD.

workshop. Those who wish to know more can read Marcia Brechtel's book, *Bringing It All Together*, or take a GLAD workshop. Instead, I have attempted to explain those principles I perceived as underlying the kinds of instruction teachers presented and to describe the strategies I saw being used in a number of elementary classrooms.

Teaching Principles

Principle I: Thematic Units

A basic principle driving the instruction in all classrooms I visited was that content should be taught in comprehensive thematic units that might last for several weeks. Most of the themes teachers chose were broad enough that instruction could cross traditional boundaries between subjects and were not bound to a single time or place. One such theme was The First Global Economy, which I saw being taught in the fifth-grade classrooms of two teachers who planned together. The unit started with an examination of production and trade in Europe and the Far East in the sixteenth century and ended with the economic and human conditions that led to the Civil War in the United States. It also included studies of the Spanish explorers and invaders who went to Central America and of slavery in North America.

Principle II: Multimodal Presentations

Another basic principle teachers followed was that any new material has to be introduced and reinforced through several modes of communication. At different times, teachers used pictures; oral explanations; physical demonstrations; electronic media; charts and diagrams; reading aloud; poems, chants, and songs; and artifacts to make the concepts, facts, and new vocabulary of the unit clear to all their students. Teachers also made available a broad range of books on the topic being studied, written at different reading levels, so that students could complement teacher-led presentations with their own reading.

All of the charts, maps, lists, and diagrams constructed were left in place throughout a unit, so that teachers could review them in their entirety with their classes or refer to parts of them as needed. Because

English-Only Teachers in Mixed-Language Classrooms

chants, poems, and songs are viewed as the most powerful tools for helping students to retain vocabulary and information, teachers had their students chant, sing, or recite them often enough that they soon memorized them.

Principle III: Oral Interaction

Teachers believed that frequent, purposeful talk about content, ideas, and work processes helps ELLs acquire both practical and academic English. The teachers I observed designed almost all classroom activities to include short verbal interactions between ELLs and their English-speaking counterparts. For longer conversations, connected to the completion of assignments or projects, teachers used partners, table teams (which, as explained in Chapter 2, are made up of mostly native English speakers, advanced ELLs, and one or two newcomers), and project groups organized to bring together the varying skills of different students.

Principle IV: Student Multimodal Expression

Teachers encouraged students acquiring a new language to express themselves in a variety of modes, just as the teachers used multiple modes to explain new material to their classes. When planning assignments, projects, or tests, the teachers I observed provided opportunities for ELLs to use drawings, diagrams, multiple-choice answers, simple sentence structures, and language support devices (e.g., word walls, student-created dictionaries) to communicate what they knew about the topics being studied. Newly arrived ELLs were allowed to use their native language for writing for a while, but as time went on they were expected to use more and more English, supplemented by the other modes of expression mentioned earlier.

Principle V: Integration of ELLs' Cultures

Whenever possible, elements of ELLs' own cultures were integrated into the themes and units being studied. The teachers assumed that in history, geography, literature, and the arts, ELLs would have information from their own backgrounds that English-speaking students did not know about. They were continually on the lookout for possibilities to present this information and made special efforts to encourage ELLs to take advantage of them. ELLs told stories or drew pictures about life in their native countries and frequently brought in pictures, books, and artifacts from home.

Use of Strategies

Not all the strategies I learned about in the GLAD workshop showed up in the classrooms I visited. Moreover, several teachers regularly used strategies that they themselves had devised. Still, I consider their creations and variations a great compliment to GLAD. These teachers had grasped the basic principles they had been taught and were using them to produce new strategies. Described in the following sections are the most frequently used and most effective strategies I observed.

Strategy I: Songs, Raps, Poems, and Chants

Rhythmic, rhyming summaries of thematic vocabulary and content were perhaps the most noticeable feature of GLAD-inspired teaching. Some of the chants I saw teachers use in their units had been taken directly from the GLAD sample units distributed at the workshop or from Marcia Brechtel's book, but others were created by the teachers themselves. I was able to recognize the patterns or melodies of many of the chants and songs I heard because they had come from familiar young children's songs and nursery rhymes, such as "The Farmer in the Dell" and "Twinkle, Twinkle, Little Star." But others were unfamiliar to me. They sounded like the raps that are so popular among teenagers today or chants that soldiers use when marching in formation. I also had the feeling that others were derived from African music sung by African slaves as they labored in the fields of the American south.

Figure 6.1 contains an example of a science chant, called a *bugaloo*[2], that was a very popular form used at all grade levels. Seeing how much students enjoyed the chants and remembered the information in them, I was easily convinced of their educational value. Clearly, they were an engaging and effective teaching device.

---

2. Different teachers used different spellings of this word.

Figure 6.1   A science bugaloo for grade 5

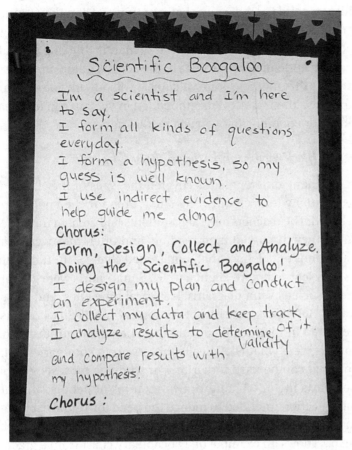

I later discovered that chants and songs worked for high school students as well as elementary students when I observed a high school history teacher having his class sing about imperialism while he played his guitar. Too few traditional classrooms take advantage of these elements of popular culture that appeal so strongly to students.

Strategy 11: Partner Talk

Discussions between students were a prominent feature in all the classrooms I visited. When teachers asked important questions that did not have right or wrong answers, instead of calling on those who raised their hands first, they would say to the class, "Talk to a partner for thirty seconds and decide what you think." Then they would call on three or four sets of partners to give their ideas. The advantages of this strategy, as I see them, are that it demands thinking and talking from every student, involves ELLs in the activity going on, and shows all students that their ideas are valuable. I will not provide an example here because there are several embedded in vignettes in this chapter and in other chapters that you will readily notice.

Strategy III: Process and Vocabulary Charts

Charts of many different kinds covered the walls of the classrooms I visited, usually leaving only one small area for the chalkboard or whiteboard. The teachers and their students had created most of these charts as they discussed their reading, and often they were marked with additions or deletions that represented changes in student thinking as they learned more about a topic. Some charts were graphic organizers, such as Venn diagrams, historical time lines, and story plot diagrams. But others were lists of vocabulary words that students had encountered in their reading or that teachers had introduced orally. Still others were what GLAD calls *process grids*, summaries of information that can be used for writing or studying for tests. Almost all of the charts included hand-drawn pictures of people, animals, or objects in action intended to reduce the need for verbal explanations and help children remember the meanings of the words on the charts. Figure 6.2 shows an example of a vocabulary chart from a grades 1–2 classroom. The definitions were not provided by the teacher, but were developed by the children from their growing understanding of the words as they read and discussed plants.

Of all these charts I found the process grids most helpful in enabling children to organize, use, and remember information. A process grid has a title that identifies the general topic, categories running across the top of the chart, and others down the left side. An example of a process grid for early American colonies is shown in the photo in Figure 6.3.

By reviewing a process grid frequently as they acquire new information, children can add to or modify the information already on the grid. Ultimately, a grid can serve as a device for studying for tests, preparing for a written report, or working on a group project. Figure 6.4 shows a completed project produced by a small group from the information in the process grid in Figure 6.3.

English-Only Teachers in Mixed-Language Classrooms

Figure 6.2   A vocabulary chart in a grades 1–2 classroom

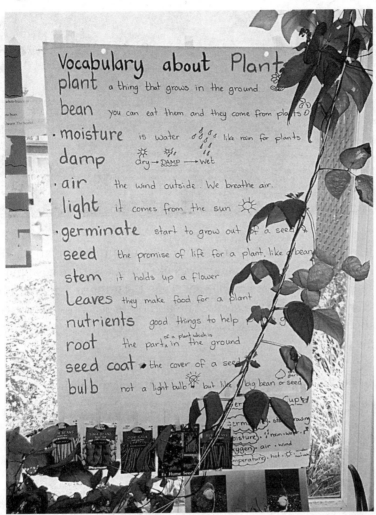

Strategy IV: Background Knowledge

All the teachers I observed presented students with a great deal of background knowledge for a new unit in various modes before asking students to do any reading, research, or writing on their own. To impart that knowledge, they read material aloud, showed pictures, gave an oral overview, displayed artifacts, and introduced the reference sources available in the classroom. They were also very diligent about explaining new vocabulary, whether the word was integral to a

Figure 6.3   A process grid for early American colonies

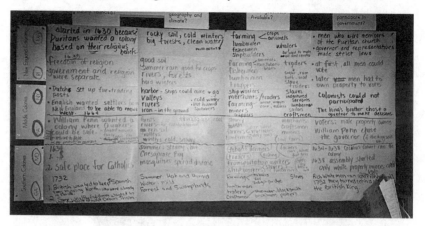

unit or simply a useful term that came up in conversation. One teacher that I observed several times liked to dress up in costume for any new history or geography unit. This was not just a gimmick but also a way of setting the scene. She and other teachers encouraged students to construct and use objects that fit into the time and place of the unit.

Figure 6.4   A group project on early American colonies

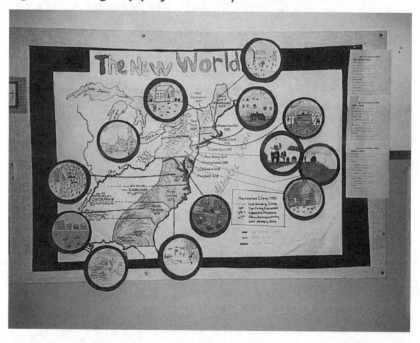

English-Only Teachers in Mixed-Language Classrooms

Classroom Vignettes

The best way to show how the principles and strategies I have just described played out in classrooms is to offer vignettes of teachers using them and students responding to them. So I offer four vignettes, one from a first-grade classroom, one from a third-grade classroom, and two from different fifth-grade classrooms (see Vignette 6.1 below, Vignette 6.2 on page 76, Vignette 6.3 on page 80, and Vignette 6.4 on page 81).

Choosing only a few vignettes for this chapter was very difficult because children were learning so much important content in every

Vignette 6.1

First Graders Work on Vocabulary

For the past two weeks, Doug Gordon's grade 1 class has been reading nonfiction books about birds from all over the world individually and in their reading groups. Today, as one group meets, Mr. Gordon asks them to look through the book they have just read silently and jot down any words they don't understand. There are five children in the group and three of them are ELLs.

After a few minutes, the teacher asks the children to name their words so he can list them on a chart that already has several words on it from previous books. Next to most of those words, Mr. Gordon has drawn little pictures to help the children remember what they mean. Today he adds six new words:

- claws
- snatch
- webbed
- feathers
- prey
- swamp

Starting with the first word, Mr. Gordon asks the children to turn to someone nearby and talk about what they think the word means. After about thirty seconds, he calls on Carlos and Enrique to give the answer they have decided upon. Carlos says, "Claws are like the bird's hand, only they more sharp."

Immediately, Annette waves her hand, and Mr. Gordon says, "Let's hear what Annette and Donna think."

Annette says, "Well, we think they're not really hands because they don't have fingers. But they work pretty much like hands," and she demonstrates by opening and closing one of her hands like a claw.

The other children in the group think both answers are right. "Good thinking, everyone," says Mr. Gordon. "How did you figure out what claws are, Carlos and Enrique?"

"Because they the big thing in the picture," Enrique answers.

continued

The children do well with most of the other words except for *snatch* and *prey*. They think *snatch* might mean eat because that is what the bird in the picture looks ready to do. "I don't think so," says Mr. Gordon. "Look at me, everybody. I'm going to snatch Ellen's book." And he does. "Snatch it back, Ellen," he says. She imitates the teacher's action and everybody laughs. Mr. Gordon quickly draws a small hand pulling a book away from another hand on the chart.

The picture on the page where the word *prey* appears is no help. It shows a large hawk flying over a nest with eggs in it and looking down. The children guess it means eggs, tree, or bird, but the teacher says, "No. Prey is some small or weak animal or bird that gets caught and eaten by a bigger animal or bird. But I don't know how to draw it."

Carlos volunteers. He draws a large bird on top of a small bird next to the word *prey*. To help all the children remember the word, Mr. Gordon suggests that Carlos and Enrique act it out, with Carlos as the prey. The two boys run twice around the classroom until Enrique catches Carlos and hauls him off into a corner, where he pretends to bite him and makes eating sounds. The rest of the class looks on, somewhat startled. But soon the others look away and go back to work. After all, Mr. Gordon pulls off tricks like this all the time.

Vignette 6.2

Learning About Native Americans

Sheryl Lindley's third graders are well into a unit on Native Americans. To begin the unit, they composed a chart that outlined what they already knew and what they wanted to know about these peoples. Ms. Lindley brought about twenty new books into the classroom that told about different tribes and their ways of living. She introduced each book by displaying it and describing its contents. She then set these books out for individual research and background reading.[1] During the course of the unit, Ms. Lindley used several articles and a commercial unit about Native Americans. In addition, she dug up some old textbooks and had the whole class read short sections from them. Information from all of these sources was combined into songs and chants about various tribes that the teacher wrote the lyrics for. One of the songs, sung to the tune of "If You're Happy and You Know It, Clap Your Hands," appears in Figure 6.5.

For the past few days the class has been reading, discussing, and dramatizing some Indian legends in preparation for writing their

---

1. These are the books Ms. Lindley considers the best ones of the group: *Arrow to the Sun*, by Gerald McDermott, *The Native Americans Told Us So*, by Melvin Berger, *The Ojibwa Indians*, by Bill Lund, *The Hopi*, by Allison Lassieur, and *The Cheyenne*, by Allison Lassieur. She also used some commercial materials: A unit called *Native Americans*, by Teacher Created Materials, Inc., *Native Americans: Cooperative Learning Activities*, by Mary Strohl and Susan Scneck, and short sections from old textbooks.

Figure 6.5   Hopi song lyrics

Hopi Indian Song

(Sung to the tune of "If You're Happy and You Know It, Clap Your Hands")

Hopis lived in the desert
Yes, they did.
They built homes called pueblos
Yes, they did.
They were made from rocks and clay,
Kept them cool on those hot days.
They built them on the mesas,
Yes they did.

They grew corn, squash, and beans,
Yes, they did.
They ground up the corn,
Yes, they did.
They made piki bread to eat,
Killed rabbits for some meat.
They worked very hard,
Yes, they did.

They grew cotton to make their clothes,
Yes, they did.
The men wove cloth,
Yes they did.
Cotton clothes kept them cool
'Cause they didn't have a pool.
Oh, they made their own clothes,
Yes they did.

Hopis made kachina dolls,
Yes, they did.
They believed they were spirits,
Yes, they did.
They made pots of clay,
Danced with snakes on special days.
They sang and made music,
Yes, they did.

—Words by Sheryl Lindley, third-grade teacher

continued

own legends. As they go over each legend, Ms. Lindley emphasizes the characteristics of legends, so that the children will be able to stay true to the genre in their own writing. Already they understand that a legend gives a magical explanation for a common situation in nature and that it starts with the way things were in the past and then goes on to tell how they changed to the way they are now.

Today the class begins with three reading groups acting out legends they have read. In each group of four or five children, one serves as the narrator and the others perform the actions of the characters and supply short pieces of dialogue. Although the performances are not very polished, the children are able to read their lines successfully and portray the plots of the legends accurately.

Next Ms. Lindley introduces three new legends to the whole class. The first one, which is the easiest, is read aloud in chorus by different sections of the class. The legend is about animals capturing part of the sun to light up the dark side of the world. The teacher reads the second one aloud, which is the Shoshone version of how the three stars came to be in Orion's Belt. In reading the legend, which tells of two antelope hunters and the trick that the wife of one of them played, she stops at different places in the story to discuss the words *myth*, *antelope*, and *plains* with the class. She tells them, "You have to know what these words mean or the story won't make sense."

All the children seem to know the meaning of *plains* since they just finished studying the Plains Indians. Several children offer ideas of what an antelope is, and together, the class figures out a pretty accurate description, which Ms. Lindley then sketches on the whiteboard. A boy named Wyatt volunteers the meaning of *myth*, which he learned from his personal reading of Greek myths.

After finishing the legend, Ms. Lindley has volunteers act out the parts where the hunters pursue the elusive antelope and the wife puts antlers on her own head to fool her husband and his friend.

The class has only a little time left to begin reading the third legend in their groups. The difficulty in this legend, which explains why there are differences in climate and topography in various regions of North America, is that weather and seasons of the year are personified as giants. Not only does Ms. Lindley want her students to understand that each giant represents an element of climate, but she also wants them to get the idea that personification of natural elements is a characteristic of legends. She hopes they will use this device when they write their own legends.

I read Anthony's legend, presented in Figure 6.6, when I returned to the class several days later. I have not made any corrections on his original manuscript.

Figure 6.7 shows Ms. Lindley, some of her students, and a couple of the charts they made during the unit.

Figure 6.6 Anthony's legend

Long, long ago there was a beaver in the path. The Native Americans stepped on his tail. The beaver said, "ouch!" And the Native Said, "Did you hear that?" They looked and looked "who said ouch?" The Beaver said "down here," he said, "You stepped on my tail and made it flat." They picked the beaver up and said, "we are sorry for stepping on your tail." Is there anything that will make you happy?" The beaver said "ok, take me to your village and give me some sticks to build my house." That is why beaver have flat tails. The End

Figure 6.7 Ms. Lindley and her students

Vignette 6.3

Learning the Language of Mathematics

Today's math lesson in Heather Smith's fifth-grade classroom is a review of the concept of comparing fractions. The class has been working on these comparisons for several days, making sure that the diagrams they are using to represent wholes are roughly the same size, so that when they are divided into fractional sections, comparisons will be accurate. Now, Ms. Smith is inviting various children to come to the front of the room to use an overhead projector to show and tell how they figured out which of two fractions is the larger part of a whole. For each child's demonstration, Ms. Smith has already printed the two fractions to be compared on a transparency.

When Lisa, a native English speaker, is called to the front of the room, the fractions to be compared are five-eighths and three-tenths. She begins by drawing two long, narrow bars (representing wholes), one beside the other. Then she says, "I'm going to divide one of these bars into eighths and one into tenths." She carefully draws vertical lines that divide both bars into the proper number of sections. After darkening five of the sections in the first bar, Lisa says, "This is five-eighths." On the second bar she darkens three sections, saying, "This is three-tenths." At this point everyone can see that the darkened portion of the first bar is larger than that of the second. Lisa finishes her demonstration by saying, "Five-eighths is bigger than three-tenths because it covers more area." This is the language format that Ms. Smith has taught the students and practiced with them. All stu-dents are expected to use it in presenting the solutions to their problems.

For the next problem, Carlos, a native Spanish speaker, is called to the projector. The fractions he has to work with are six-sevenths and eight-ninths. Before he can begin, Ms. Smith asks if anyone wants to guess which fraction is larger. The class recognizes that this is a harder problem than the first because in both fractions the number representing the part is so close to the number representing the whole. Yet a few students are willing to make guesses. Ms. Smith accepts their guesses as good thinking and says, "Let's see."

Carlos does not guess; instead he confidently begins his demonstration. Like Lisa, he draws two bars, but he is very careful to make them longer than hers and to put one exactly above the other. Although he doesn't explain this strategy, it appears that he realizes that a comparison will be difficult if the diagrams are not accurate. Still without speaking, Carlos divides the first bar into seven reasonably equal sections and the second into nine sections. In the first bar he darkens six spaces and then says, "This is six-sevenths." He darkens eight sections on the second bar, saying, "This is eight-ninths." Although the difference in fraction sizes is small, Carlos' careful drawing has made it possible to see that the second is indeed bigger than the first. He concludes his demonstration using the same sentence format as Lisa: "Eight-ninths is bigger than six-sevenths because it covers more area."

The Age of Exploration

For the past week teacher Linda Spangler has been working on a unit called The Age of Exploration with her fifth-grade students. Today Ms. Spangler's class is practicing a chant (see Figure 6.8) that includes information about the Vikings, northern European explorers, and the Spanish conquistadors.

After going through the whole chant, which is printed on a large chart in front of the room, the teacher folds it to expose only

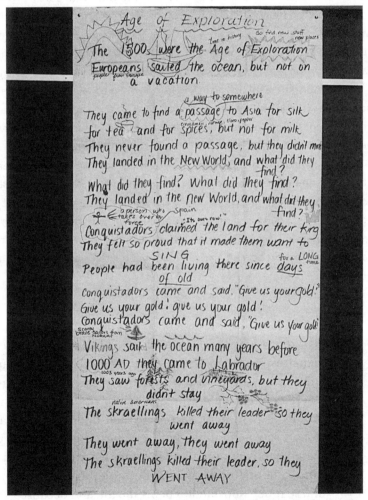

Figure 6.8   Chant for the Age of Exploration unit

continued

the part about the conquistadors. She explains that the word means conquerors in English and that the groups that came from Spain came primarily to take the land and its valuable products rather than to explore or settle it. She also explains who the Aztecs were and that their king was Montezuma. Over his name on the chart she draws a small crown to help them remember who he was. She also draws little symbols over other new vocabulary words, such as *gold, architecture*, and *religion*, for the same purpose.

For about ten minutes she explains that part of the chart and asks students questions to check their attentiveness and understanding of what she has been explaining. One child asks the meaning of *spread* in the phrase "spread their religion," and another wants to know what *occupy* means in the phrase "occupy the Aztecs' land." Ms. Spangler demonstrates as well as explaining by spreading imaginary peanut butter on bread and pre-

tending to push a child out of his chair in order to occupy it.

Having completed her explanation, the teacher reads aloud the first paragraph from a social studies textbook that tells the same story and mentions the leader of the Mexican conquistadors, Hernan Cortes. She asks the students to work with partners to read the rest of the story (only one page in length) and write down information for a process grid they will construct to summarize information about all the New World explorers. On the grid they will have five categories to fill in with brief phrases for each man. The categories are personal background, sponsor motives, dates, route of exploration, and impact.

As the students work, Ms. Spangler and an aide move among the groups to keep them on track and explain any other words they do not understand. After the chart is completed, the students will work in small groups to write summaries about the explorers featured on the grid.

classroom I visited. In addition to the lessons I describe in these vignettes, I observed parts of a world history/geography unit that stretched over two or three centuries and at least four continents. I saw science units going on at different grade levels, with children performing experiments, recording their findings, and drawing conclusions. I saw math units that were meaningful because children were manipulating numbers and fractions using objects, visual demonstrations, and oral explanations. Because there were so many concepts and so much information being taught, and because I saw only single lessons of most of these units in my visits, I was unable to write accurate or meaningful vignettes about them.

ELLs and English-Speaking Students Learning Together

7

Outside of the initial small groups that introduce basic English vocabulary and sentence structure, ELLs should be working side by side with their English-speaking classmates. What they need most is the practice, support, and challenge that come easily and purposefully through interactions with their peers. ELLs should be included as active participants in any class work in the content areas.

Teachers who have worked before with newly arrived ELLs may well wonder if this is a realistic expectation. In their experience, they may have found these children were overwhelmed by a new school, new classmates, and an unfamiliar language. Most of the time, the newcomers parroted what their classmates were saying and imitated what they were doing. Although they may have understood some of what was going on in class, their teachers had no way to tell for sure. Eventually, the more diligent ELLs began to participate actively in class work, but others found the passive role so comfortable and readily accepted that they stayed in it for the rest of the school year and, often, well beyond.

Despite the validity of this picture of ELL functioning in some classrooms, I have seen a far different picture in most of the classrooms I have visited. From observing teachers who provide the kinds of support described in Chapters 4, 5, and 6, and who use grouping and partnering creatively for content-area activities, I have become convinced that ELLs can work productively in regular classrooms right from the beginning. That does not mean that newcomer ELLs can contribute as much work or do as well as English-speaking students in their first year, but that they can put in their fair share of time and effort, add quality to group products, and take away substantial learning in both content areas and English. In this chapter I attempt to explain and illustrate how classroom teachers can design various kinds of activities that will allow ELLs to participate with their classmates to the full extent of their abilities.

In elementary classrooms, teachers typically use four different organizational structures for giving instruction and providing for student work. They are

- whole class
- small group
- tutor and tutee
- individual

Carefully designed and managed, these structures can provide students of all abilities with enough support to enable them to read, write, speak, listen, plan, solve problems, create projects, review information, rehearse presentations, and even take tests. Let's look now at how ELLs can participate in the kinds of classroom work that might be expected under each structure.

Whole-Class Activities

Typically, elementary teachers use a whole-class structure for giving directions, presenting new content material, and going over completed assignments. They also sometimes use it to have students review for upcoming tests or correct short-answer tests already given. If required to work alone in these situations, most ELLs cannot do what is expected of them. They miss too much of the teacher's explanations and directions and forget some of the vocabulary that has been taught. But when children are partnered for whole-class activities—each ELL with an English-speaking student—many teachers

English-Only Teachers in Mixed-Language Classrooms

have discovered that both types of students understand more and do a better job.

During a presentation of content material, as described in Chapter 6, the teacher pauses at suitable places to give partners time to talk over what they have heard and seen before asking them to respond to her questions or take action. This kind of partner talk encourages careful attention to the teacher's words and demonstrations and makes every student—not just the ones called upon to answer questions—responsible for thinking about the information presented and using language to explain his thinking. In addition, ELLs get an interpretation of the teacher's words from their partners, extra time to think, and the opportunity to rehearse what they want to say before volunteering to speak.

When teachers give a lengthy assignment to their classes, partnering is also a valuable support system for ELLs. After giving instructions, the teacher can say, "Turn to the person next to you and talk about what I just explained. Make sure that both of you know what to do, how to do it, and when it is due." Then, instead of asking, "Does everybody understand?" she can call on a few sets of partners to see if they have questions. If they do, their questions are likely to be the same questions others have been wondering about.

When working with a partner, ELLs are also better able to go over homework, review information previously taught, and correct short-answer tests. Again, what an ELL doesn't get from the teacher's explanation, he has a better chance of getting from his partner's repetition in simpler language. He can also ask his partner questions that he may not feel comfortable asking in front of the whole class. If the partner doesn't know the answer either, both may feel more confident to voice their question openly.

Along with using partnering extensively, teachers need to provide extra support to ELLs in whole-class activities. In reviewing material for an upcoming test, for example, you can provide support by giving information in more than one form. You may prepare a written set of questions about key concepts in a unit, along with a list of important vocabulary words for the class to consider, and accompany the written outline with diagrams or pictures. After giving partners time to talk over the material you have provided, you can reexplain the most important points, clarify word meanings, and answer any questions. In this process, ELLs get to review material that will be on the test four different times in four different ways: reading it, viewing it, discussing it, and hearing interpretations from other sets of partners and the teacher. Vignette 7.1 on page 87 illustrates how two teachers who work as a team prepare their students to take a science test on the planets.

In my view it is also desirable for partners to share test taking occasionally. Not only do ELLs need some support in this process, which may be very different from what they are used to, but also both students can benefit from the truth in the old adage "Two heads are better than one." When partners agree right away on an answer, one writes it down for both of them. When they disagree, they can talk it over and, perhaps, reach agreement. If that doesn't happen, each partner can write her own answer and initial it. Although a partnered test may not give a clear picture of each child's knowledge, that seems to me to be a minor concern compared with the inherent benefits of collaboration. As long as teachers do not use such tests as the defining measure of each child's learning, they are a valuable addition to the array of assessment tools teachers have at their disposal.

Small Groups

Small groups, whether working on reading, writing, or a content area, give ELLs the same benefits of explanations, shared ideas, assistance, and correction as partnering gives in whole-class activities. But small-group work offers further advantages by providing assignments selected for the abilities and interests of the group members, broader and more intense collaboration opportunities, and closer attention from the teacher to what each student is doing.

For the sake of all students, not just ELLs, group members should work together on assignments. That means that you have to teach them how to collaborate, help each other in various ways, and trust each other enough not to interfere in a task others are already working on. This kind of teaching involves demonstrating roles—yes, more than once—guiding practice, and having independent practice sessions with feedback from you and other students.

Vignette 7.1

Preparing for a Science Test

Before giving an end-of-unit test on the solar system, both Heather Smith and Linda Spangler review with their fifth-grade classes the information they will be expected to know to meet state standards. The teachers are well aware that the concepts of this unit have been quite difficult for all their students, but especially for the ELLs, who have had to learn a large technical vocabulary.

Throughout the unit the teachers have worked hard to make the content comprehensible by using visual representations of the planets and their relations to the sun, physical demonstrations of planetary movement, and repeated use and explanation of key vocabulary words, such as *revolve*, *orbit*, and *elliptical*. Children have been encouraged to use these words, too, in asking or answering questions. The class has also constructed a process grid with the name of each planet down the side and five columns listing the characteristics of each planet. In addition, the teachers have created a chant that includes both vocabulary and information that have been taught. The chant is posted on a large chart in front of the classroom, and the teachers have drawn small pictures or symbols between the lines to help students remember the meanings of difficult words. The class practiced the chant aloud frequently when the unit was being introduced and now reviews it from time to time. Without being required to do so, the students have memorized it easily because of its rhythm and rhyme.

In the final review students are asked to name planets and categorize them by their structure and distance from the sun. In Figure 7.1 (p. 88), Ms. Spangler reviews information about the planet Mars.

The students use model sentence structures that their teachers have presented previously and fill in the blanks:

> The four rocky planets are _____, _____, _____, and _____.
> The four gas planets are _____, _____, _____, and _____.

Students also complete a Venn diagram on the chalkboard that provides a visual organizer of the differences between inner and outer planets and also their commonalities. This diagram will help them study for the test.

On the test itself, students will have to label illustrations, make Venn diagrams, and draw pictures of the planets with written explanations beside them.

Afterward, when I asked the teachers how their ELLs had done on the test, they told me that their drawing, labeling, and categorizing within a Venn diagram were just fine. They did not do as well on their written explanations.

The test is reproduced in Figure 7.2 (p. 89).

continued

Figure 7.1   Teacher Linda Spangler reviews information for a science test on the planets

continued

Vignette 7.1 ***Continued***

Figure 7.2 Solar system test

Name ____________________

Date ____________________

Solar System Celebration of Knowledge

Word Bank:

Sun	Moon	Pluto	Neptune
Earth	Mars	Mercury	Jupiter
Uranus	Saturn	Venus	rotation
day	inner	year	revolution
outer	rings	moon	asteroid belt
gases	rocky core		atmosphere
hydrogen	helium	methane	oxygen
nitrogen	gravity	orbit	temperature
carbon dioxide		elliptical	sunrise
sunset	noon	midnight	

1. Draw and label a picture of our Solar System in order. Include all the planets (include rings) and the asteroid belts. When you have drawn and labeled all required objects, then add moons and other real objects in our Solar System for extra credit.

continued

2. Illustrate and explain what causes Earth to have periods of light (days) and periods of dark (nights).

3. Explain what causes Earth to have years.

4. Objects in our Solar System have regular orbits. Illustrate how the Sun, Earth, and Earth's moon orbit.

continued

5. There are two kinds of planets in our Solar System.

The rocky planets are: The gas giants are: Other outer planets are:

_____   _____   _____

_____   _____   _____

_____   _____

_____   _____

6. Use the diagram below to show how the inner planets are similar to the outer planets and how they are different.

Inner planets   Outer planets

continued

Vignette 7.1 *Continued*

Bonus Questions:

- Pluto was, until recently, the farthest known planet from the Sun. How is it like the other planets that are far from the Sun? How is it different?

_____

_____

_____

_____

_____

_____

_____

_____

_____

_____

_____

_____

_____

- Earth has gravity. Explain how it helps us.

_____

_____

_____

_____

_____

_____

_____

_____

_____

_____

_____

_____

_____

_____

_____

Typically, small groups are assembled to work on daily assignments or long-term projects that proceed without close teacher supervision. Both types of work involve a number of responsibilities to be shared among the group members, and both require some structuring. For a daily assignment, structuring usually means no more than figuring out who does what. Although students in a small group are capable of deciding that for themselves, there is a good chance that the ELLs in the group will get to do the drawing, lettering, or some other easy part of the job, while the English-speaking students do the reading, writing, and thinking parts. As the teacher, you could make the work assignments or let the students draw straws for them, but it is probably just as good to be watchful and suggest to a group that Alberto write the explanation this time.

With long-term projects, more work and more planning are necessary. A group needs a well-defined structure beforehand and a plan for doing the work and bringing it all together. Thus, each group should include workers of different abilities and ELLs, and each should have a strong leader. Within the group children may work alone at times, with a partner, in a cooperative, or as a whole body. A partnership is, of course, two students working together; a cooperative is made up of three or four students who advise and help each other; the whole group does the planning; and the leader assigns tasks and monitors their progress. It follows, then, that in order to cover all the tasks required and to ensure that there is work enough for everyone, a small group must have six to eight members.

Considering the many responsibilities of a group working on a project, I have some recommendations about who should do what and where ELLs best fit in. The chart displayed in Figure 7.3 outlines the ideal apportionment of tasks in a hypothetical group of eight students with three ELLs in it.

Although the students in a group should decide who fills each role, you should be present during this process to oversee their decisions. You can be frank—but also diplomatic—in giving the reasons you think that Alba should partner with Susan and that a particular four-person cooperative should not have three ELLs in it.

Figure 7.3   Work apportionment chart

Apportioning Work for a Long-Term Project

TASKS	PERSON(S) ASSIGNED
Selecting group leader	Teacher or entire group
Deciding what end product will be	Entire group
Assigning tasks	Volunteers and group leader
Generating questions to complete tasks	Cooperatives
Finding information in reference sources	Partners
Reading and discussing articles, stories, or chapters	Partners and individuals
Writing descriptions, explanations, captions, and so on	Partners and individuals
Locating photos or illustrations	Individuals
Drawing maps, pictures, or diagrams	Individuals
Reviewing finished tasks	Cooperatives
Monitoring individual and group progress	Group leader
Organizing the completed tasks into project form	Entire group
Presenting the completed project	Cooperatives, partners, and individuals

Creating Simplified Reference Books for Future ELLs

An ideal long-term project for a small group is making an easy-to-read reference book for a science or social studies unit as a supportive aid for ELLs to come. As I mentioned in Chapter 2, level 1 and 2 ELLs often experience difficulty trying to read grade level textbooks because of their large vocabulary loads and abstract writing style. When teachers try to provide simplified texts for their ELLs, they usually find that there are few on the market and that those few, written for young children, leave out much important information.

Working together, a small group of English-speaking and ELL students can do an effective job of putting together such books. After working on a unit with their teacher, they know what the important information for their grade level is and how to express it clearly and simply. They know what illustrations are needed, and they have their own notes and charts to use as examples. Moreover, they are aware of the trouble spots and extraneous information in the materials they used, and thus are in a good position to smooth out the former and omit the latter. Finally, these students are highly motivated to produce something useful that will be read and appreciated by ELLs for years to come.

The extra benefit of such a project is that it puts ELLs in the important position of decision makers. They are best qualified to decide whether English-speaking group members have explained concepts clearly, whether they have included all the important information, whether they have defined new words meaningfully and in context, and whether they have included a sufficient number of illustrations. Although ELLs are not the best copy editors, they are the best judges of content and style.

The Emphasis on Partnering

By now it should be clear that I believe the key factor in enabling ELLs to produce work of value in any situation is partnering. With research, questioning, writing, or projects, newcomers need support in figuring out processes that other group members are already familiar with, and they need to be able to turn to someone beside the teacher for assistance. As ELLs become more competent in English and more knowledgeable about group processes, they can become the partners for newcomers and take on leading roles in small groups. In addition, they will be able to contribute more high-quality work to the group, especially if the assignments the teacher gives open opportunities for them to use the content and background knowledge they have brought with them from their own cultures. In this way a further benefit of small-group work is the opportunities for ELLs to shine.

Tutoring

Even when partnering is the primary structure in a mixed-language classroom, there are times when a tutor-tutee arrangement between students is a necessary support for ELLs, especially when the vocabulary is extensive and technical and the textbooks are not well written. If you tend to think that tutoring is a heavy and profitless burden for English-speaking students, remember that a significant body of research indicates that student tutors learn as much or more than their tutees. Furthermore, tutoring between classmates is not the same as teaching. Tutors do not present new material; they assist ELLs in locating, interpreting, or organizing material that the teacher has already presented or that the class has read. They also help them take notes, review for tests, and practice vocabulary or spelling.

As long as tutoring is for a specific purpose and provided as friendly support, the tutee will have no reason to feel inadequate and the tutor no reason to feel superior. A clever teacher will also try to provide opportunities for ELLs to be tutors—either for younger children or for classmates who are learning something about an ELL's language or culture. Such situations are great self-esteem builders for ELLs, who always seem to be the ones on the receiving end of help, and that self-esteem will carry over into other learning situations.

One final word of advice about partnering and tutoring is that both roles need to be frequently rotated among the English speakers in the class. Because some children are by nature more patient and nurturing than others, all ELLs should have the chance to work with those who do a good job.

Working Alone

Despite all the benefits of children working together, there come times in every classroom when each child must work alone. Recreational reading, writing about a personal experience, a letter, or an opinion, and taking a test to demonstrate learning are situations that come to mind. When ELLs work alone, they may need modifications in their tasks and some other ways to get the support that partners and tutors provide in other situations. The most important modification for ELLs is having a good supply of comprehensible reading materials available in the classroom at all times: reference books, fiction and nonfiction books, magazines, newspapers, comic books, and books created by former students who worked on the same units. Although ELLs can usually find appropriate books on their own, especially if all books are labeled for level of difficulty, they may sometimes need help. From working with these students in formal reading groups, you can estimate their reading competence and suggest books within their range that will also fit their current interests.

When books and children are well matched, ELLs shouldn't need further support to read them. You should gently discourage ELLs from asking for help every time they encounter an unfamiliar word by letting them know that we all—children and adults— manage to read books without knowing every word in them. You can tell your ELLs that they may ask a friend for the pronunciation of a word or the meaning of a phrase if they really need to, but if they can get the general ideas of a text without knowing one or two words on a page, that's OK. They should just skip the unknown words and keep on reading.

Modifications for writing and tests are mainly matters of limiting quantity and complexity; deciding how much original writing is reasonable for students at different levels of English competence, and determining at what point you should expect more than short declarative sentences from them. At the same time, you should let all your students know that three clear, heartfelt sentences are better than two pages of blather.

On tests of content subjects, the difficulty of questions should increase systematically, so that you can say to level 1 and 2 ELLs, "Honoree, Elmondo, and Vittoria, do only numbers 1 through 4; Vladislav and Oswaldo, do 1 through 7; everyone else should do all ten questions." *Difficulty*, as I am using the term here, means not only the complexity of the questions but also whether they require marking a statement as true or false, drawing a diagram, filling in a blank, or writing a long original answer.

On both written papers and tests, ELLs should be allowed to draw what they can't explain in words, as Atzary, a fifth-grade girl, did in the assignment shown in Figure 7.4. In addition, errors in spelling and grammar and the use of a limited vocabulary should not be counted against ELLs. Teachers should base their grades—if they must grade such work—on the student's quality of information, thinking, creativity, and organization.

Another way to modify writing assignments in content areas is to allow ELLs to write about subjects that have been thoroughly discussed in class or about material they have read, while referring back to the original material or their notes. They should also be able to look again at pictures and objects used to provide background knowledge on a topic. In addition, they should have vocabulary lists with definitions and drawings readily available. With these types of modifications, children have a familiar stock of information at their disposal and do not have to grope for words to explain it.

When doing creative or personal writing, ELLs can use literary models, as described in Chapter 5, as the foundation for describing their own experiences or creating different forms of imaginative stories.

Finally, when students are very new to this country, it may be best for them to write in their native language for a while or to supplement their meager stock of English words with words from their own language or small drawings. Although the written pieces that result may be difficult for you to comprehend without a translator, it is still worthwhile for the writers to attempt to express themselves in a written language rather than do busywork.

Patience Pays Off

I hope I have not given the impression that the grouping arrangements and strategies suggested in this chapter will quickly convert your ELLs into competent English speakers, readers, and writers. Unfortunately, I suspect you will not see your work and theirs come to fruition in as little as one year, unless they were already fairly adept

Figure 7.4 "How Baby Dolphins are Born and Raised"

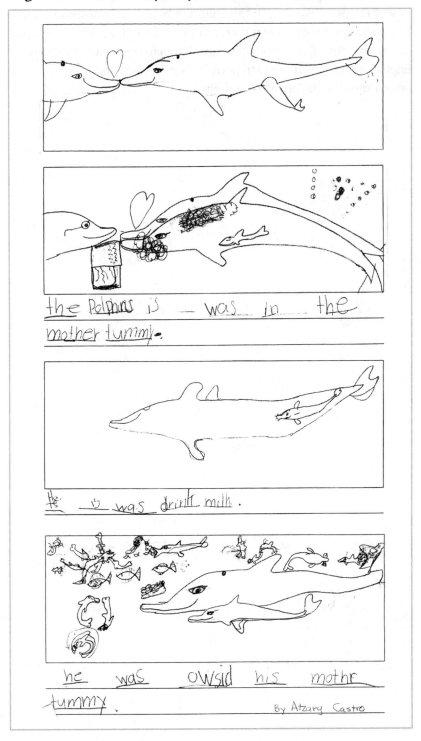

the Polphins is — was in the mother tummy.

He is was drink milk.

he was owsid his mothr tummy.

By Atzary Castro

in academic English when they arrived in your classroom. The advice in this chapter, like that in the chapters before it, is not intended to be a panacea. Rather, it is merely a supply of language life jackets that will enable your ELLs to begin swimming in foreign waters, allow your English-speaking students to perfect their strokes, and keep you from drowning while trying to save them all.

Providing Further Support for ELLs 8

One commonly voiced objection to the practice of teaching ELLs in English is that it demeans their native languages and cultures, undervalues the skills and knowledge they have acquired in those languages, and reduces their status to that of second-class citizens in their new school community. Critics cite the rigidity of classrooms where students are forbidden to speak or write in their native languages. Additionally, they say that schools are practicing discrimination when they isolate ELLs in special classrooms for most of the day or teach them from textbooks intended for much younger children. Where these things are happening, I think the critics are absolutely right.

Nevertheless, I do not believe that trying to make the children of nonnative families fluent in English as their second language is discriminatory or harmful. The children I've talked to certainly don't think so. I've found that even the youngest ELLs in various schools understand that English is the language of public intercourse in the United States. They know that they will have to be able to read, write, and speak English well in order to get good jobs and participate fully in American society, and they do not resent those facts. All they want is some leeway to speak their own language among friends, to use it in school at times when the effort to use English becomes too much, and to feel that their culture is valued by their teachers and classmates. In this chapter I examine the possibilities for creating the school, classroom, and community conditions that make ELLs feel accepted, equal, and, at times, privileged while they are learning English.

In Chapter 2, when I described the preparations for the ELLs who may enter your classroom, I suggested several ways to help them understand what was going on in class, meet their most basic needs, and connect them with their English-speaking peers. In addition, in Chapter 3, I described continuing activities that would help ELLs form and maintain their social relationships. What I have neglected so far are suggestions for bringing ELLs' cultures and languages into the classroom and involving their parents in their socialization and learning.

Including ELLs' Cultures in Classroom Activities

Let's begin by taking a second look at the mixed-language classroom to see what teachers can do to make ELLs feel they are necessary and important members of the class. However, one caution is necessary at the outset: Don't overdo things by planning events in which only one ethnic group stands out. For example, why celebrate the Chinese New Year or Cinco de Mayo if you are not doing anything about holidays from France, Italy, other foreign countries, or the United States? Efforts to single out one ethnic group for special attention may turn out to be embarrassing for members of that group or offensive to other students who feel that their ethnic origins are worthy of some attention too.

This particular problem can be avoided by noting the holidays that all your students would like to celebrate on the classroom calendar and planning to do some small event on each of those days. Suggest this at the beginning of the year and give your students some time to talk to their parents and come back with the names, dates, and purposes of two or three holidays they think should be celebrated at school. Then those students will be responsible for planning those celebrations, with your help and the help of their parents, of course.

Another way to approach cultural celebrations is to have some large inclusive events at various times during the year. There could be a Cultural Foods Day each month on which several children sign up to bring in an ethnic food for everyone to taste. Or you could plan a Roots unit in which students research their ethnic backgrounds and prepare a display and a short talk for their classmates. If this works out well, the presentations could become a traveling show for other classrooms in the school. A third possibility is to have a schoolwide All Our Holidays celebration that includes presentations, displays, and/or costumes representing all the ethnic groups in the school. Right before either the winter break or the spring break would be a good time for such an event and that would help the school avoid controversies over Christmas and Easter celebrations.

Beyond celebrations, there are many other opportunities for students to share their cultures and their special related skills in the classroom. Why not have some brief language lessons periodically, in which ELLs teach the class and you such things as numbers, the alphabet, or a few useful sentences in their native languages? If some members of the class seem especially interested in any of these lessons, they could start a Russian, Spanish, or Swahili club that meets during the noon hour for them to learn more words from that language and practice speaking them.

A similar type of activity would be to have ELLs share a book that reflects some aspect of their culture. The book need not be written in a foreign language, but if it is, the sharer could read a paragraph or two aloud so classmates can hear how the language sounds. Then he could give a brief summary of the rest of the book in English.

Since most of what I have suggested here is aimed at older ELLs, here are a few things younger children could do:

bring an artifact from home for show-and-tell

sing a song or recite a rhyme in their native language

teach classmates a game from their home country

make a display of family photos (This works especially well as part of a child's birthday celebration at school.)

draw pictures of their original home or people dressed in native clothing

write about or draw their family, explaining or illustrating their work, recreation, and other daily activities

Whenever feasible, all students in the class, not just the ELLs, should be encouraged to participate in the activities suggested in this chapter. Their cultures and families are worthy of attention, too.

Finally, I want to remind you that your ELLs at any level of English competence are capable of carrying out important roles in the class social structure. To strengthen their self-confidence, it might be wise to give them routine responsibilities at first, such as handing out or collecting materials, but they should be moved up the line of responsibility as soon as they show they are able to handle it. Both they and their English-speaking classmates learn an important lesson when they see that leaders come in all colors and from all ethnic groups.

Although valuable learning experiences are included in everything suggested in this section, the activities are essentially socializing events intended to integrate ELLs into the classroom community and make apparent their skills, knowledge, and social standing. But we must remember that we are concerned with more than social matters in a school setting. We have to do some serious thinking and planning to allow ELLs to shine in academics, too.

Expanding Academics to Include ELLs' Interests

The approach that comes first to mind is to teach history and geography units at each grade level that involve the countries your ELLs come from. This is a great idea, but, unfortunately, not always possible. In these days of high-stakes testing, most school districts have fixed curricula that must be taught at each grade. And with so much emphasis on test preparation, there is little or no time left for supplementary studies that would focus on the backgrounds of ELLs. So, what can you do to infuse the language and culture of your ELLs into the units you must teach?

In most periods of American history, a number of people from other countries or cultures had important roles in signal events. It is not difficult to find the names of outstanding figures from the same backgrounds as your ELLs who were instrumental in American wars, geographical expansion, the arts, science, or politics. The lives and accomplishments of these people should be highlighted (as well as those of Native Americans) when attention is given to famous Americans of

English-Only Teachers in Mixed-Language Classrooms

the time. In units on the geography of other countries, doing the same is not so easy. Often the country being studied bears no relationship to your ELLs' origins and is of no particular interest to them. (Of course, this may also be true for your English-speaking students.) There is no point in trying to create connections where none exists; teach the unit straight and look for your opportunities elsewhere.

That elsewhere may very well be in literature, music, art, or current events. When your class is doing work in any of these areas, consider the possibility of having some students read, write, and /or draw about outstanding people in that field. As part of your picture file, keep a special section on famous figures of the past and current celebrities, along with short biographical articles about them. Here's a suggested list of the kinds of pictures and information you will want to collect for children to use.

    artists from different time periods
    artists representing different styles or forms of expression
    well-known writers of the past and present
    famous composers
    prominent sports figures
    movie, music, dance, and drama celebrities
    political figures
    inventors
    humanitarians
    business leaders
    educational leaders
    prizewinners in any field

If no famous person in your files fits naturally into your classroom studies, don't worry. It's OK to skip Picasso or the Beatles in any given year. On the other hand, if even one child expresses an interest in a famous figure or a celebrity, allow her to do the bit of research necessary to find a picture and some biographical information and report to the class. A good time for such a report may be as part of the morning rituals or the daily read-aloud time.

Not for one minute do I think I have exhausted all the possibilities for bringing ELLs' cultures and languages into the classroom, but I hope I have given you enough start-up ideas to bring out your own ingenuity and the vast knowledge of your ELLs.

Bringing Parents into the Picture

Forming positive relationships with parents begins even before their children come to school. That is the time for welcoming letters, posters in public places, home visits, and invitations to visit the school. Because time and money are limited, teachers or principals can't do everything I suggest here, but they can choose a few activities that seem right for them and their community and follow through on those.

I think the easiest introductions are letters of information that may be mailed to the families you know are coming or distributed through religious institutions and community organizations, which are likely to meet newly arrived families before you do. These letters should include the name and address of the school, the starting date of the school year, school hours, bus schedules, school registration procedures, a list of basic student supplies, and the names of the principal and office personnel, with annotations next to the name of anyone at school who speaks a language other than English. If possible, the letters themselves should be translated into the languages newcomers are likely to speak. In addition to the letters, a good idea would be to put up posters with basic information in local stores and other places newcomers frequent. The posters should tell people where to go for further information.

A more time-consuming, but also more rewarding, activity would be to hold welcome meetings with refreshments at houses of worship, community centers, or the school. Again, having translators on hand would be a big advantage. In addition to giving the information already mentioned, the principal could introduce teachers and tell the grades they teach. Incidentally, these meetings should not be restricted to ELLs' families, but should include all families new to the school.

The most valuable type of welcome is a personal visit to the homes of new students. Obviously, these visits can be very time consuming and probably would have to be done on the teachers' own time. Yet I know several principals and teachers who make visiting the homes of ELLs a ritual every year during the first few weeks of school, and I know one pair of kindergarten teachers who set out with a red wagon filled with new books and go to the homes of all incoming kindergartners to say hello and deliver a free book to each child.

Just as you work to sustain social relationships with children throughout the year, you should do the same with parents. There are many occasions for inviting parents to school and many opportunities for communicating with them at home. If, in addition, you can enlist them as classroom helpers, they will be better able to understand their children's schoolwork and help—or at least encourage—them to do it.

Following is a list of ordinary school activities that can also be occasions for inviting parents to be guests or to participate.

PTA meetings
parent-teacher-student conferences
field trips
end-of-unit celebrations (with displays of student work)
back-to-school night
class play, poetry reading, or other types of student performances
exhibits of children's artwork and/or writing
birthdays or holiday parties

You may find that it takes personal invitations to get some ELLs' parents to attend these events. The reason may be that they are working at their jobs when the events are held, that they are embarrassed about their less-than-perfect English, or that they come from cultures in which parents are not really welcome at school.

The greatest human assets you can hope to find are bilingual parents who are able to help you communicate with other parents. They can also work side by side with those parents who are reluctant to volunteer because of their weak English skills. But there are powerful technological assets at your disposal too, primarily your camera and your computer. Take lots of pictures of ELLs working, speaking, or demonstrating in front of the class and interacting with other students. Also, photograph some of their work that has been displayed around the room but is not likely to go home. Send copies to parents by computer or with the child. If possible, attach the photos to blank sheets of paper on which both you and the student can write a short message.

Special Events

In addition to the customary school events, try to plan some that will be especially appealing to ELLs and their parents. More important than appeal, though, is involving parents in their children's education. Your primary objective is to plan events in which ELLs and their parents can be the central actors, not just observers. Following are some possibilities. A few have been mentioned earlier as ways to involve students; now think of them as ways to get parents working with their children at home and performing with them (or assisting them) in the classroom.

> family roots displays
> ethnic games day (instead of the traditional field day near the
>   end of the school year)
> ethnic dance or music performances
> cooking demonstrations
> demonstrations of a native craft
> language lessons
> ethnic holiday celebrations
> a student-and-parent-constructed geography quiz
> showing of a foreign movie with English subtitles

If you can schedule any of these events in the evening rather than during the school day, you will greatly increase the chances of getting working parents to attend.

Another important way to keep parents involved is sending home a regular newsletter. In it, you should not only report on classroom events and studies but also ask for parent help and suggestions. Create a special section that is the equivalent of the help-wanted section of a newspaper. Ask for a variety of things and types of assistance—everything from donating scraps of cloth to volunteering to help out for half a day every week. When it comes to volunteering, be specific. Many parents who are willing to decorate a bulletin board do not feel competent to correct children's math or spelling papers.

In your newsletter, try to include children's names and photos along with information on their accomplishments (but not reports of grades, please), such as a list of everyone who handed in all homework on time or those who were noticed doing something nice for someone else. On the other hand, putting in examples of children's work can make a newsletter too large or single out only the most gifted students for attention. It is better to mention any new display of children's work in the classroom and invite parents to come in and see it.

Listed earlier under ordinary school activities was parent-teacher-student conferences. I believe that all such conferences should include the students whose work and behavior are being discussed. They have the right to hear what their teacher's and parents' perceptions are and the right to express their own perspectives. In addition, many ELLs are capable of acting as translators or interpreters between their teacher and their parents. Although this is usually a benefit, it could be a disadvantage if either side needs to discuss a problem that the students should not be informed about in this manner, such as a divorce or special education testing. In such a case it would be better to have a disinterested adult translator on hand. Perhaps you could enlist a relative, neighbor, church member, or social service representative for this job; if not, ask the parents if they know someone who could act as a translator. If, despite everyone's best efforts, a translator cannot be found, you should put the important information about the students' performance in writing and give it to the parents to take home. I am certain that a concerned parent would then be able to find someone who could translate a written report that is clearly important.

Going the Extra Mile

I have left for the end of this discussion the suggestion that teachers need to move toward ELLs' parents all year long, instead of expecting that parents will come to them. By *move toward*, I mean sending notes and making phone calls and, more important, going off school grounds to meet parents where they live and where they gather. Typically, ELLs' parents are not assertive. Most of them will say and do nothing even when they feel strongly that things are not going well for their child at school. This habit serves children, teachers, the school, and the parents themselves badly. The best hope you have of breaking the habit is to become a frequent, friendly presence in their community: someone who listens, cares, and helps. In suggesting that teachers go this extra mile for their ELLs, I am breaking away from the pattern I have tried to maintain throughout this book of showing you ways to teach and support your ELLs without adding extra burdens to your already overburdened professional life. I do that now because, in the end, your students, as well as you, must survive in a bureaucratic system that provides little support for either of you. Only you and the parents you inspire can walk the extra mile with these children who have such great needs and such great promise.